William E Ku[...]
715 Meade Stre[...]
Johnstown, PA 15901

Copyright © 2020
Published by the Daily American
All rights reserved. No part of this work may be reproduced or used in any form or by any means, graphic, electronic or digital without written permission of the Daily American, 334 West Main St., Somerset, PA 15501, 814-444-5900.

Table of Contents

Acknowledgements	3
I. Introduction	4
II. A Brief Discussion of Johnstown's Beginnings	6
III. Johnstown Post 1970	27
IV. From the 100th Anniversary of the Great Flood to the Mid 90's	32
V. Johnstown from the mid 1990's to post 9/11	35
VI. The Great Recession and Beyond	39
VII. Seeing Johnstown Through New Eyes – County Health Rankings	52
VIII. Disparities Between Johnstown and the Rest of the County	85
IX. Documentary Filmmakers Descend Upon Johnstown	100
X. Running for City Council and The 2018 Midterm Election	105
XI. Activists Working to Turn the City Around	111
XII. A Social Media Profile of Johnstown	131
XIII. The Literary Scene in Johnstown	141
XIV. The future of the City/Region	160
About the Author	163
References	164
Appendices	173
Index	176

Acknowlegdments

I want to thank the Richard Burkert and Andrew Lang of the Johnstown Area Heritage Association, Larry Blalock of Put People First and the Unity Coalition, the people at the Cambria County Library, the Johnstown Creative Writing Connection, and Ian Williams for their assistance in writing this book. I would also like to thank my father Thomas Ricci for his support while I wrote the book. Lloyd Stires, Michael Giazzoni, Jessica Maniccia Smith, and Nick Brisini were helpful in editing this book. Thanks to Eric Luden for the great cover art.

I: Introduction

This book is a look at those in Johnstown who are down and out. It looks at the large scale publicly available numbers for the city and the area and the stories of those struggling to make ends meet. The city was once a thriving steel city with 67,327 residents in the 1920s but in 2018 had 19,447. It was the third fastest shrinking city in the U.S (Census Bureau, American Community Survey, 2017). It has endured three major floods, the closing of steel mills, and an opioid epidemic. The city now has the seventh highest poverty rate in Pennsylvania (Sauter, 2019).

Johnstown and Cambria County were once a Democratic stronghold but Donald Trump carried the county with 67% of the vote in 2016. In the year after the election documentary filmmakers, including Katie Couric, flocked here to look at why there was such a turnaround. This is a look at the city from the inside. It is not a fluff piece on the city.

Johnstown in a sense is a city not unlike other mid-size rustbelt cities. Donald Mitchell in his Master's Thesis *A History of Homelessness - A Geography of Control: The Production of Order and Marginality in Johnstown, Pennsylvania* (1989) states:

> "...Johnstown may stand as a metaphor for the historical production of landscapes of control throughout the United States. The historical geography of control and marginality in Johnstown is also the historical geography of control and marginality in Industrial America."

In the years prior to the 1923, the city's steel industry was under local control. Later it was bought up by Bethlehem and U.S Steel. The city would later pay for its lack of control.

The later chapters are longer as there is more recent data available. I give historical facts to place the numbers in their appropriate context. This is not a comprehensive history of the city. The census bureau and other state and federal agencies have a wealth of information on the city. Statistics allow us to see patterns that are not easy to see with the naked eye.

II. A BRIEF DISCUSSION OF JOHNSTOWN'S BEGINNINGS

Figure 1, A statue of Johnstown's founder Joseph Johns (originally Joseph Schantz) and the author

The story of Johnstown is the story of the Industrial Revolution. It was founded in 1770 by Joseph Schantz, a Mennonite from Switzerland who later Anglicized his name to Joseph Johns. He placed the city at the confluence of the Little Conemaugh River and the Stonycreek River to form the Conemaugh River. It is a two hour drive from Pittsburgh and a one hour drive north of the Mason-Dixon Line. The Conemaugh River was named after the Conemaugh Indians who had lived on the land previously. The city is often called a miniature version of Pittsburgh, is also at the confluence of two rivers, is surrounded by the Allegheny Mountains, and had a long history of steel making. It was incorporated as a borough in 1800 and as a city in 1889 after the great flood (Johnstown, PA Website).

Figure 2, The Feeder Canal Building located where the Pennsylvania canal once was. The mural depicts the canal.

In the 1830s the state of Pennsylvania wanted to have a canal to equal the success of the Erie Canal in New York State. The Pennsylvania Canal was built to connect Philadelphia to Pittsburgh to have an all water route to the Mississippi River via the Ohio River. Johnstown was a stop on the canal. The area's iron and coal could easily be transported to the interior of the U.S. (Coleman, 1985). A special rail system had to be built at Cresson, PA to get the canal boats across the Allegheny Mountains. Charles Dickens stayed in Johnstown on a tour of the U.S. in the 1840's (Johnson, Giles, & Michaels, 1985). According to the book Johnstown: The Story of a Unique Valley, Johnstown was a stop on the Underground Railroad going back to at least 1837 (Johnson & du Pont 1985).

The canal did not last, as the railroad made it easier to cross the Allegheny Mountains, but the area's coal and iron was still in demand (especially during the Civil War). Welsh immigrants came to the area followed by Eastern and Southern Europeans to work in the Cambria Iron Works. The city had its largest percentage increase in population in the 1860 Census, from 1,269 in 1850 to 4,185, a 229% increase. In 1874 there was a lockout, where the owners of the Cambria Iron Works refused to let the workers in. As a result, the workers of the Cambria Iron Works failed to unionize (Williams and Yates, 1985). The United Mine Workers were more successful in organizing the coal mines during this period (Williams and Yates, 1985). The second largest percentage gain in population in Johnstown's history occurred in the years between 1880 (pop. 8,380) and 1890 (pop. 21,805), 160.2%, despite one of the greatest man-made disasters in U.S History.

Flooding

Figure 3, A house damaged by the 1889 flood

Flooding had always been a problem in the Flooding had always been a problem in the Conemaugh Valley with the town being at the same level as the city's rivers. This was made worse when the South Fork Fishing and Club, whose membership included some of the richest men in Pittsburgh like Andrew Carnegie, Henry Clay Frick, and Andrew Mellon, rebuilt an abandoned earthen dam north of the city to create their own private lake. No engineer was consulted in its redesign. The owners of the club refused to expand the spillway as they were concerned about fish escaping from the lake.

On May 31, 1889 the dam burst releasing a 30 foot high wall of water that picked up debris following the Little Conemaugh River and bursting into the city like a tsunami. Debris piled up on the old stone bridge and later burned when the water receded. Bodies, presumably from the flood, turned up in the Ohio River as far away as Cincinnati, OH. An estimated 2,209 people were killed (McCullough, 1968). Only 9/11 was worse as a man-made disaster in U.S. history in terms of the death toll (Encyclopedia Britannica). After the flood Johnstown was chartered as a city in December of 1889 (Kagan, 1985).

In a referendum at the end of the year the surrounding municipalities of Cambria, Conemaugh, Millville, Prospect, Woodvale, Coopersdale, and Grubbtown were consolidated with Johnstown. Franklin and East Conemaugh voted not to consolidate and remain outside the city to this date. Grubbtown is located in what is now the 8th Ward of the city. You can see the vote totals in Figure 4. In the 1890 census, the city's population increased to 21,805 from 8,380 in 1880 due to the annexation of surrounding communities and in spite of the flood the year before.

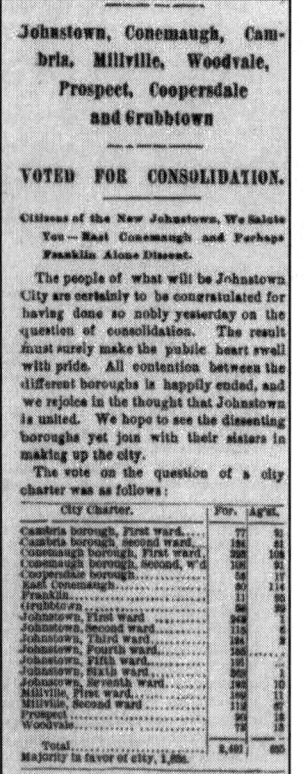

Figure 4, The vote totals from the 1889 referendum on consolidation with the City of Johnstown

Donald Mitchell's Master's Thesis on the homeless in Johnstown is titled *A History of Homelessness – A Geography of Control: The Production of Order and Marginality in Johnstown, Pennsylvania (1989)*. He writes that survivors of the flood moved into shanties on the hillsides for years afterward despite "exhortations to the homeless by health and military officials to move to the tent cities on the valley floor." The shanties remained for a few years afterward.

Figure 5, Cleaning up at the Stone Bridge after the 1889 flood

Johnstown was able to rebuild from this tragedy and the town continued to grow until 1920 when it peaked at 67,327 (Mitchell, 1989). Part of the reason for this growth is due to the city annexing the surrounding municipalities, such as Moxham in 1898 and Roxbury in 1901 (Whittle 2005, p. 18). The adjacent boroughs lost population from 1890 to 1900 during this period, from 8,502 in 1890 to 7,868 in 1900 (Morawska, 1985a, p.86).

The Inclined Plane was built in 1891 to rescue flood

victims (Figure 6). An Inclined Plane is also called a funicular, which is a train designed to climb a steep hill. The streetcar system was expanded to reach Windber to the south of the city in 1902 (Coleman, 1985). The Cambria Iron Works was bought out by Bethlehem Steel in 1923 (Whittle 2005, pp 56-58). Unfortunately, the city's problems with flooding were not over. Floods would occur again in 1894, 1907, 1924, 1936, and 1977 with major ones in '36 and '77.

Figure 6, The Inclined Plane was built in 1891 to save citizens from flooding

African Americans in Johnstown

In the early 1800's, Johnstown Borough was a stop on the underground railroad line running from Cumberland, MD to Lake Erie. Daniel Morrell (head of the Cambria Iron Works) and William Slick were supportive of aiding escaped slaves. Two brothers who escaped slavery in Virginia in 1837, settled the Borough. In 1860, Morrell instructed his employees to vote for Abraham Lincoln for president (Sutor, 2019e). A law was passed in Pennsylvania calling for the gradual abolition of slavery in 1780 but it was not completely eradicated in the state until the 1840s (Finnerty, 2019b).

The book *Johnstown's Nineteenth Century African American History Primer* (JAHA, 2003) looks at the census records for African Americans from 1850 to 1900. In 1850, there were 33 African Americans living in Johnstown Borough, 2.6% of the population. Four worked as a blacksmith, four as a laborer, four as "probably a servant," and three worked as a barber. By 1860 the number had increased to 66 but the percentage of the city's population decreased to 1.6%. Nine worked as a barber, three as a laborer, four as a stone mason, two as a factory girl, one as a flat boatman, one as a clergyman, one as a domestic, and one as a woolen factor.

By 1870, the number of African Americans decreased to 41 in the city, 0.5% of the population. Twelve worked as a servant/housekeeper which was the most common occupation. In 1880 the number rebounded to 209, 2.5% of the population. The most common occupations were 22 as a servant/housekeeper; 21 worked as a laborer. One did work as a fire fighter.

The 1890 census numbers for African Americans were not included in JAHA (2003) book but the numbers from the 1889 city directory listing African Americans in the city are. 124 were listed as living in the city. Of these 53 were listed as dead or missing in the 1889 flood, 42.7% of the total African American population for the city. Nine were confirmed dead in the flood, 7.3% of the total. It's unknown how many of the missing were dead. Was there a higher proportion of missing among non-white residents of the city?

In the 1900 census there were a total of 314 African Americans. This is a 190% increase from 1889, which is a far greater increase than the 65.8% increase in the city's general population over the same period. The African American population of the city increased to 462 in 1910 but then nearly quadrupled to 1,671 in 1920 as many African Americans and Mexicans were recruited to come to the city to work in the steel mills during World War I (Whittle, 2005, pp. 162-163). My grandfather and his brother, Italian immigrants, came to the city during this period.

In 1923 there was an incident where an African

American man killed four police officers (McDevitt, 2020). The mayor of the city then, Joseph Cauffiel, responded to the incident by ordering every African-American and Mexican who had been living in the city since 1916 to leave the city. They were living in the Rosedale section of the town at the time. African Americans were prohibited from holding public gatherings (Craig, 2014). Some 2,000 did leave the city. However, the African American population eventually recovered and there was a slight increase in the city's African American population to 1,768 by the 1930, a net increase of 97 (Sherman. 1963; Morawska, 1985b; McDevitt, 2017; McDevitt, 2020).

White flight from the city did begin after this period (Morawska, 1985b). Cauffiel, a Republican, served as Mayor from 1920-1924. He was reelected again in 1928, but went to jail before he could finish his term in 1931 for two years for extortion, perjury, and gambling (Johnstown Café; Whittle, 2005, p. 206). He was later pardoned by Governor Gifford Pinchot.

The number of African Americans decreased slightly to 1,595 in the 1940 census (Morawska, 1985b). African Americans generally lived in the Rosedale section of town during this period (Whittle, 2005, pp. 162-163).

The documentary film *We'll Make the Journey* (Williams, 1992) includes 17 interviews of African Americans whose parents were part of the great migration from the south to Johnstown in search of better opportunities during World War I and the 1920s. They discussed how they were relegated to the hotter jobs in the blast furnace. The interviewees did say that the conditions that they found in Johnstown were better than what they left behind. The documentary did not discuss the incident with Joseph Cauffiel and Rosedale because those who were interviewed had arrived in the city after the incident. It also erroneously stated that African Americans had been in Johnstown since 1870 when they were in reality here long before the Civil War.

As the city's population began its decline in 1920, the surrounding communities such as Richland, Ferndale, and Westmont (collectively known as Greater Johnstown) continued to grow from 50,205 in 1900 to 97,495 in 1920 to 112,586 in 1960 (Johnson & du Pont, 1985). During this time the African American population of the city continued to increase from 314 in 1900 to 1,650 in 1920 (2.5% of the population) to 2,695 in 1960 (5.0% of the city's population). Population decline in Greater Johnstown began after 1960. The population decline in the city that began after 1920 accelerated in the 1960's in the suburbs and has continued since unabated ever since. A horse drawn streetcar system was built in the city in 1883 (Coleman, 1985). The streetcar system was steadily dismantled in the 1960's due to population changes and increased use of the automobile (Coleman, 1985).

In 1900, 20.5% of the city was foreign-born or 7,318. By 1910 this number had reached 27.8% or 15,316. In

Other Ethnic Groups in Johnstown

1900, 52% of foreign-born persons were from Southern and Eastern European countries which had increased to 66.5% in 1910. The percentage of Southern and Eastern Europeans in the foreign-born population of Johnstown increased to 79.4% in 1940 (Morawska, 1985b). Morawska (1985a) in For Bread with Butter: Life-Worlds of East Central Europeans in Johnstown, Pennsylvania, 1890-1940 thoroughly chronicles the struggles of East Central European immigrants namely Slavic, Hungarian, and Austrian immigrants in the city in the early part of the 20th century. The struggles of this immigrant group could conceivably be expected to be similar in other immigrant groups.

Morawska (1985a) found that in the steel industry

approximately 7% of East Central European immigrants who remained in the city moved up from unskilled or unspecified semiskilled laborers (as defined by the mills) in the mills to semiskilled or skilled workers from 1900 to 1920. She also looked at first generation immigrants who remained from 1915 to 1930 and at second generation immigrants from 1920 to 1949/50. These numbers are summarized in the tables below. There was generational overlap in these periods. There were not enough first-generation immigrants to follow from 1900 to 1930. First generation immigrants tended to move from city to city, especially in the early days after they arrived in the U.S.

Table 1a shows how job mobility was for first generation immigrants from 1900 to 1920 and from 1915 to 1930 and for second generation from 1920 to 1949/50. These were immigrants who remained in the city during the periods in which they were tracked in the census and the city directories. The percentages on the observed side of the table are the actual shifts of immigrants from unskilled or unspecified semiskilled to semiskilled or skilled, semiskilled or skilled to unskilled or unspecified semiskilled, and immobile (no change in employment status in the mill over the period). The expected percentages if there were no discrimination side of the table shows what the numbers that would be if the overall mobility rates were the same as they were for Western European immigrants or native workers (ergo no discrimination).

The upward mobility rates for both first generation periods were considerably lower than they were for the second generation and for the numbers we would expect if there were no discrimination. The downward mobility numbers were higher for second generation mill workers than for first generation workers and for what would be expected if there were no discrimination. The downward mobility numbers were identical for the 1900-1920 and the 1915-1930 periods for the first generation were both

Table 1a
Job mobility from unskilled or unspecified semiskilled to skilled or semiskilled steelworkers for 1st & 2nd generation East Central European Immigrants who remained in the city for the period (Morawska, 1985a, pp. 100, 164, 166)

Period	Observed %			Expected % with no Discrimination		
	Upward Mobility	Downward Mobility	Immobile	Upward Mobility	Downward Mobility	Immobile
1900-1920 First gen	7	4	89	21	2	77
1915-1930 First gen	10	4	86	20	4	76
1920-1949/50 Second gen	17	14	69	31	10	59

nearly identical to what would be expected if there were no discrimination.

Morawska also looked at the transition between blue collar and white-collar workers who remain in the area over the same period (Morawska, 1985a). For all three generation cohorts, the upward mobility was lower than would be expected if the promotion rates were the same as native workers and western European immigrant workers. There was a small increase in the upward mobility for the 1915-1930 first generation to the 1920-1949/50 second generation cohorts. There was a slight increase in downward mobility from the 1900-1920 first generation

Table 1b
Mobility from Blue Collar to White Collar Jobs and vice versa for 1st & 2nd generation East Central European Immigrants who remained in the city for the period (Morawska, 1985a, pp. 99, 163, & 165)

Period	Observed %			Expected % with no Discrimination		
	Upward Mobility	Downward Mobility	Immobile	Upward Mobility	Downward Mobility	Immobile
1900-1920 First gen	8	2	90	20	1	79
1915-1930 First gen	11	8	81	19	7	74
1920-1949/50 Second gen	12	9	79	22	8	70

cohort to the 1915-1930 first generation cohort with little change in the second generation.

Within the East Central European immigrant groups, the priests, the immigrant bankers, the merchants, the saloon keepers and the undertakers had the highest social status as white collar workers. Skilled positions were in the middle of the social milieu as blue collar and the laborers in the mill and coal miners were at the bottom of the social ladder (Morawska, 1985a, p 236).

Different immigrant groups tended to prefer neighborhoods with their own ethnic group. Often people from the same regions of their native countries lived in the same neighborhoods. The East Central Europeans lived primarily in Cambria City, Minersville, Prospect, East Conemaugh, and Franklin Boroughs (Morawska, 1985a, pp. 96-97). Italian immigrants congregated in Conemaugh Borough and Prospect. Some immigrants were scattered throughout the area. For example, former Pennsylvania Senator and presidential candidate Rick Santorum's grandfather emigrated from Northern Italy to Tire Hill, which is located just across the county line in Somerset County (Sojak, 2011).

Native born citizens with parents born in the U.S were 52.5% of the city's population in 1900. This percentage decreased to 47.7% in 1910 but gradually increased to 60.2% of the city in 1940 (Morawska, 1985b). Ku

On July 10, 1902 (only 13 years after the great flood), the Rolling Mill Mine had been active on the Westmont hillside overlooking the city for 46 years. It provided much of the coal used in the Cambria Iron Works, about 3,000 tons per day. On that day there was a powerful explosion in the mine. One hundred and twelve miners were killed, 84, or 75% of which were immigrants from England and Eastern European countries, were killed." Should be changed to "One hundred and twelve miners were killed. Eighty-four, or 75% of which were immigrants from England and

Klux Klan activity would be found in the area in the 1920s targeting African Americans, Catholics and Jews as immigrants came to the city (Johnson & du Pont, 1985). At a KKK rally in nearby Lilly a gun battle erupted between them and the local townspeople in 1924 (Craig, 2014; Whittle, 2005). Twenty-five people were shot and three were killed. The town was chosen because it was 80% Catholic (Craig, 2014).

Rolling Mill Mine

Eastern European countries, were killed. Most of the deaths were from asphyxiation. Looking at the official list of the dead, some of their ages were indecipherable. Of the ones I could decipher, the oldest of the deceased was 54 and the youngest was 16. The deceased had at least 132 children. Sixty-seven of the deceased or 59.8% were married. It ranks as one of the worst mining disasters in Pennsylvania history. The mine was closed in 1931.

The public and Catholic school system was rebuilt after the flood. In the public elementary schools in 1912, the student faculty ratio was 37 students to one teacher (Whittle, 2005, p. 112). Randy Whittle (2005, p. 110) in Johnstown Pennsylvania: A History, Part One: 1890-1936 showed that as the school age population in Johnstown increased from 1907 to 1917, the percentage of students

Figure 7, The entrance to the Rolling Mill Mine on Westmont Hill

in school decreased. This is due to the small number of students attending high school. Enrollment in high school did not increase in the 1920's (Whittle, 2005, p. 115).

Education in Johnstown

Figure 8, Johnstown High School teaching staff 1924

The Catholic school system began as the immigrant population of the city from Germany, Italy, and Eastern Europe increased (Whittle, 2005, p. 116; Craig, 2014). Johnstown Catholic High School (later Bishop McCort High School) was created in 1922 with 300 students (Whittle, 2005). These schools were created at the same time that the Ku Klux Klan was campaigning against Catholics, African-Americans, and other ethnic minorities. At its height in the 1920s the KKK was estimated to have 1,775 members in Johnstown, 2.6% of the city's population (Whittle, 2005).

The University of Pittsburgh, Johnstown campus (or UPJ as we call it) was founded in 1927. It was originally located in Moxham where the Cypress Avenue School was later located. In 1967, the campus was moved to its current Richland Campus (Whittle, 2007).

During the Great Depression, the Johnstown School District cut costs by putting a requirement for female teachers to be single (Whittle, 2005). They would be dismissed if they were married. The overall student faculty ratio (including high school and junior high) went from 24 students to one teacher in 1929-1930 to 30 students to one in 1933-1934.

Labor Struggles before and after the 1936 Flood

By 1919 the steel workers in Johnstown were successfully unionized and they struck for better wages and working hours. The overall effort was unsuccessful because the union was crushed. However, the workers did win a 14% wage increase and overtime wages of 150% of their base salary (Morawska, 1985a). African-Americans were brought into the city to help break the strike (Mitchell, 1989). From 1925 to 1929, the average monthly salary of a mill worker was $816 to $1,416 for a laborer, $996 to $1,212 for a "pick miner," $1,346 to $1,415 for skilled laborer, and $1,608 to $41,884 for a coal miner (Morawska, 1985a). The household income of immigrant families was directly related to the number of household members who were working with families earning more than $2,000 per year having a median of 3 members working. Households with less than $1,000 in income typically had one member employed (Morawska, 1985a). These earnings were $200 to $300 lower than they would have been if they worked full time during the month. In March, 1933, at the height of the Great Depression, the unemployment rate was reported to be 35.6% (Mitchell, 1989).

In 1932, World War I Veterans were promised bonuses in 1945. Due to the Great Depression, they needed their bonuses early and protested in Washington, D.C. The protest was brutally crushed by President Herbert Hoover. Johnstown Mayor Eddie McCloskey told the protesters that they could stay here in the city. They remained in Ideal Park only for four days, as there were inadequate food and services for them (Whittle, 2005).

In 1937, another strike occurred at Bethlehem Steel. Lorain Steel in Moxham was a subsidiary of U.S Steel and did become unionized at this time (Whittle, 2007). This time organizing efforts were initially unsuccessful for the steel workers at Bethlehem Steel (Williams & Yates, 1985). However, the National Labor Relations Board found Bethlehem Steel responsible for channeling money to Mayor Daniel Shields to support efforts to "vilify" the Union (Whittle, 2007). Because of these events, the organizing efforts were finally successful in 1941. The International Ladies Garment Workers Union (ILGWU) and Teamsters Unions were successful in organizing in the city in 1945 (Williams & Yates, 1985; Whittle, 2007).

The 1936 Flood

In the 1930's the city, like the rest of the U.S, was reeling from the Great Depression. On March 17, 1936, there was a large amount of snow that melted quickly, in addition to a large amount of rain. The water level in the valley gradually rose to 15 feet above flood stage. The Inclined Plane did save lives that day and only 25 people were killed, but 9,000 were left homeless and there was $40 million in property damage (Mitchell, 1989). President Franklin Roosevelt visited the city in the aftermath and directed the Army Corps of Engineers to put in flood control measures by dredging the river and by putting in concrete river walls. It was hoped that a major flood would not hit the city again.

Figure 9, Franklin Street in the 1936 Flood

Creation of the Johnstown Housing Authority

In 1943, the city's housing authority carried out slum clearance in the Conemaugh Borough, Cambria City and Prospect neighborhoods. They also planned public housing in the Oakhurst and Prospect neighborhoods (Mitchell, 1989; Whittle, 2007). Of the applicants for public housing, 106 out of 131 or 81% of applicants were approved who worked for Bethlehem Steel, 10 out of 13 applicants or 77% from other employers were approved, and three out of three applicants who were unemployed or single mothers were approved. The median income of those approved for public housing was well above that of the target populations in these neighborhoods.

In 1900 36.7% of families in the city owned their home. The number increased to 40.1% in 1930 but then decreased to 34.6% in 1940. In 1950 that percentage rose to 45.6% (Morawska, 1985a). Families often supplemented their income by taking in boarders in their apartments and houses (Morawska, 1985a). Among East Central European immigrants, home ownership among persisters (those who remained in the city) was 27% in 1920 and 35% in 1930. Among those immigrants who left and then returned to the city, it was 10% in 1920 and 16% in 1930. In 1920 the home ownership rates for immigrants were below the city-wide rate regardless of whether they were ordinary workers, skilled workers, or those working in business or services. By 1930, only those who worked in business and services had ownership rates above the city rate (Morawska, 1985a). The value of the homes owned by immigrant male skilled laborers, business and service workers was higher than for ordinary laborers in 1920, 1925, and 1930. For female immigrants who were widows or boardinghouse keepers, the values were lower for 1920 and 1930. In 1925 the values for female households were higher than for male ordinary laborers but not for the other two male worker categories (Morawska, 1985a). The most common occupation of female heads of households was homemaker (Morawska, 1985a).

Environmental Effects of Coal Mining

At the turn of the century, as coal mining became more and more common in Somerset and Cambria Counties, some mines were abandoned. As the abandoned mines filled up with water, they became contaminated with acid. The acidic water would eventually drain into the Stonycreek, Little Conemaugh, and Conemaugh Rivers and would kill all of the fish. It would be more than a century before the Conemaugh and Stonycreek Rivers would have fish in them again (The Stonycreek Website, 2008).

Post war to the 1960's

As with the rest of the U.S, Johnstown prospered during the years the baby boom generation was being born. Enrollment in the Johnstown School District began to decline after World War II by an average of 200 pupils per year until the baby boom generation came of school age in the 1950s (Whittle, 2007). The Cambria County War Memorial Arena was built on Napoleon Street. In the 1940's, Republicans and Democrats in Cambria County were evenly matched in the number of registered voters (Whittle, 2007). Unemployment in the city peaked after World War II and the Korean Wars with returning veterans but soon rebounded back to normal (Whittle, 2007).

The city's first television station, WJAC, began in 1949. The city's two newspapers, The Johnstown Tribune and The Johnstown Democrat were bought up by the same company, the Johnstown Tribune Publishing company that owned WJAC. WJAC TV is now owned by Sinclair Media. The two newspapers were merged to form the Johnstown Tribune-Democrat (Whittle, 2007).

III. JOHNSTOWN POST - 1970

The city had its largest percentage decrease in population from 1960 to 1970, declining from 53,949 to 42,476, a loss of 11,473 people, or 21.3%. At the same time the surrounding county had an 8.1% decrease from 203,283 to 186,785 for a total loss of 16,498. 70% of the decline in the county population was due to the decline in the city population. The first Vietnam veteran was elected to Congress in the U.S, John Murtha, as a Democrat from Johnstown in 1974. He would later be implicated in the Abscam scandal in the early 1980's.

The city's African American population continued to increase to 2,705 in 1980 from 1970 or 7.7% of the population while it was decreasing in the surrounding communities of Greater Johnstown from 3,377 in 1960 to 3,194 in 1980. The percentage of African Americans in the city was still below the state percentage of 8.8% in Pennsylvania and the U.S percentage of 11.7% in 1980 (Johnson & du Pont, 1985).

There have been calls for consolidating the surrounding municipalities of Johnstown with the city. There was a major attempt made in 1970 (Sutor, 2013). It would have put the city's population over 100,000 and would have brought in more federal and state money. The measure was popular in the city but was voted down in each of the 14 precincts outside the city. The often-cited reason for its defeat was that those in the surrounding municipalities did not want to give up power. Another potential reason was that they did not want to be associated with the growing minority population there.

The city reverted to a strong mayor format in 1974 with Herb Pfuhl as mayor, a Republican. In a strong mayor format, the mayor acts as the chief executive.

This was done to prevent political infighting between mayor and council and to make city government more efficient. Pfuhl would be elected to five non-consecutive terms as mayor, the longest serving mayor in the city's history.

The iconic hockey movie Slap Shot was filmed in Johnstown in 1976. The plot concerned the city losing its semi pro hockey team, the Johnstown Jets. The film starred Paul Newman and the famous Hanson brothers. It remains the most famous movie filmed there to date and it is a metaphor for what the city would become. Bethlehem Steel, in an internal study (Mitchell 1989), had decided to close its plant in Johnstown but the next flood temporarily put a damper on that.

1977 Flood

Figure 10, Aerial view of Johnstown after the 1977 Flood

In 1977 the third major flood hit the city. On July 20 a microburst (an extreme rainstorm) stalled over the city and dropped 12 inches of rain in 10 hours. Five dams failed. These dams were smaller than the South Fork Dam in 1889. The flood claimed 84 lives. Many businesses, including the Penn Traffic department store (Jeshonek, 2015), closed and never reopened.

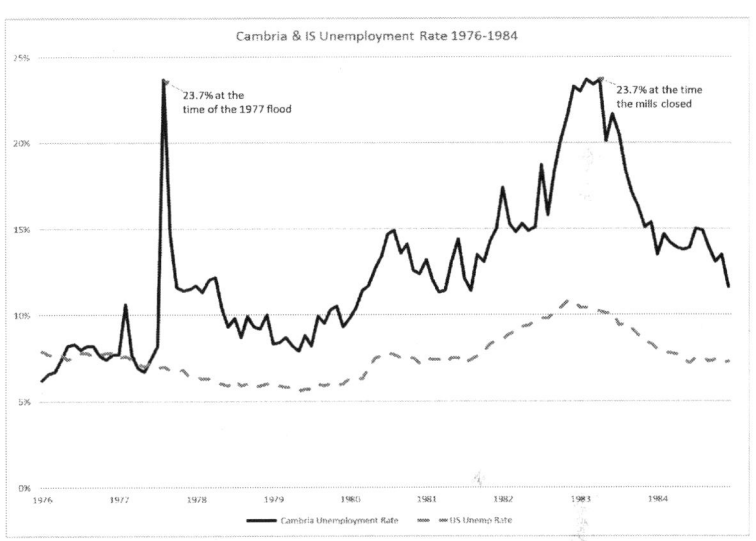

Figure 11a-Monthly Unemployment Rates for Cambria County (PA) (source PA Department of Labor & Industry)

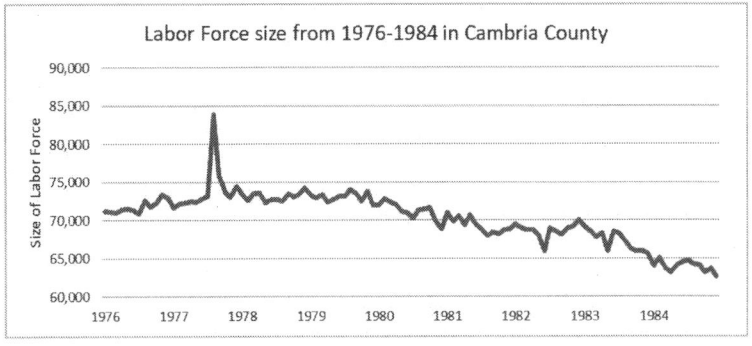

Figure 11b, Change in the labor force in Cambria County (Source: PA Department of Labor & Industry)

As the city was recovering from its third major flood, the steel mills were closed. This gave the county a 23.7% unemployment rate in Jan 1983. This was the highest rate in the U.S at the time and equaled the highest rate immediately after the 1977 Flood. The rates in 1977 and 1983 were surpassed only by the peak in the rate during Great Depression (Mitchell 1989). The white unemployment rate in 1983 was 16.5% while it was 52% for African Americans (Johnson & du Pont, 1985). While the overall unemployment rate decreased in 1984, the size of the labor force likewise decreased as can be seen in Figures 11a and 11b. Figure 11b shows that this decrease occurred due to the unemployed leaving the county and thus were no longer included in the unemployment rate.

An interracial couple was murdered in the city by racist Joseph Paul Franklin in 1980 on the Washington Street Bridge. The killer confessed to using a high-powered rifle on wooded hillside. He was put to death in 2013. This was part of a killing spree that ran from 1977-1980 and took about 12 lives (Wikipedia, n.d.).

From 1970 to 1980 the city's population decreased by an additional 16.4% from 42,476 to 35,496 for a total decrease of 6,980. Cambria County as a whole only had a 1.9% decrease from 186,785 to 183,263 for a total decrease of 3,522. This suggests a gain for the county outside of the Johnstown city limits in the 1970's of 3,458.

Another film was made in Johnstown in the aftermath of the mills closing. All the Right Moves starring Tom Cruise (pre Top Gun and post Risky Business), Craig T. Nelson, and Lea Thompson. Cruise's character is a high school football player struggling to escape a life in the steel mills by obtaining a scholarship to play college football. It temporarily brought some money into the economy.

The city also relied on other sporting events such as the All-American Amateur Baseball Tournament (AAABA) to bring in cash every August. As with the rest of Western Pennsylvania, Johnstown had its share of sports stars such as Pete Vuckovich who won the American league Cy Young Award pitching for the Milwaukee Brewers. Artrell Hawkins played for the Cincinnati Bengals and the New England Patriots while his brother Andrew Hawkins played for the Cincinnati Bengals and the Cleveland Browns. Carlton Haselrig was a champion wrestler in high school and college who was drafted by the Pittsburgh Steelers and made the Pro Bowl. Larod Stephens-Howling played for the Arizona Cardinals. Finally Jack Ham won four Super Bowls with the Pittsburgh Steelers and was elected to the Pro Football Hall of Fame.

IV. FROM THE 100TH ANNIVERSARY OF THE GREAT FLOOD TO THE MID-90S

1989 was the 100th anniversary of the Great Johnstown Flood. The Papal Nuncio (the Vatican's ambassador to the U.S) came to the city and said Mass at St. John Gualbert Co-Cathedral. Lee Iaccoca visited the city and spoke at Sunnehanna Country Club. Jon Bon Jovi gave a concert at the Point Stadium. Johnstown received a new minor league hockey team called the Chiefs. It was named after the fictional hockey team in the movie Slap Shot. An Oscar winning documentary film was made on the flood by Charles Guggenheim.

Frank Pasquerilla, the CEO of the Crown-American Corporation, built a new corporate headquarters for his company that owns shopping malls and hotels downtown. It was meant to be a showcase for the city to the world. Figure 10 shows that the unemployment rate improved during this period while the size of the labor force increased. Johnstown was placed in Act 47 assistance for distressed municipalities in August 1992 and has been there ever since (Sutor, 2017).

Mark Singel, a Democratic State Senator representing Cambria County was chosen as Governor Bob Casey's Lieutenant Governor in 1986. He served as acting governor while Casey had a liver transplant. In 1994 he made a run to succeed Casey as governor but lost to Congressman Tom Ridge 45% to 39%. He would have been the first Governor from Johnstown. Another Johnstowner, Peg Luksik founder of Mom's House, ran on the Constitutional Party ticket and received 13% of the vote. There was also a high-profile criminal trial, Cambria County Judge Joseph O'Kicki was put on trial and convicted of bribery and corruption (Associated Press, 1989). While awaiting a second trial he fled the country for Slovenia and spent his last days there (Roddy, 1998).

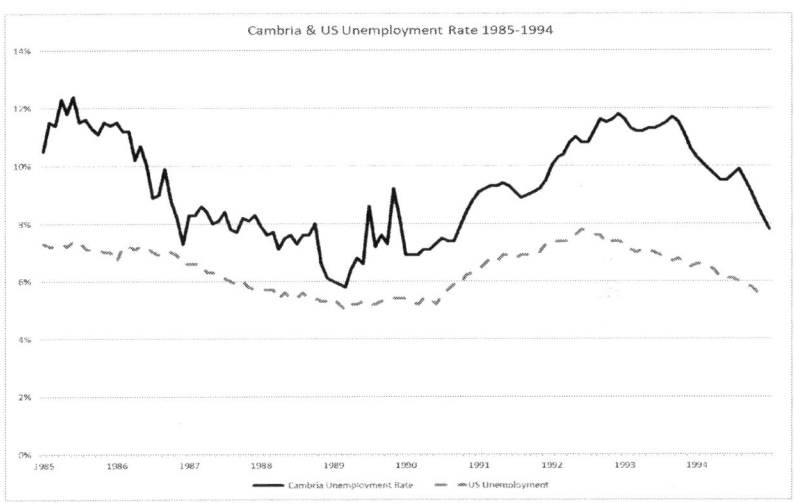

Figure 12a, Change in the Unemployment Rate in Johnstown (Source: PA Department of Labor & Industry)

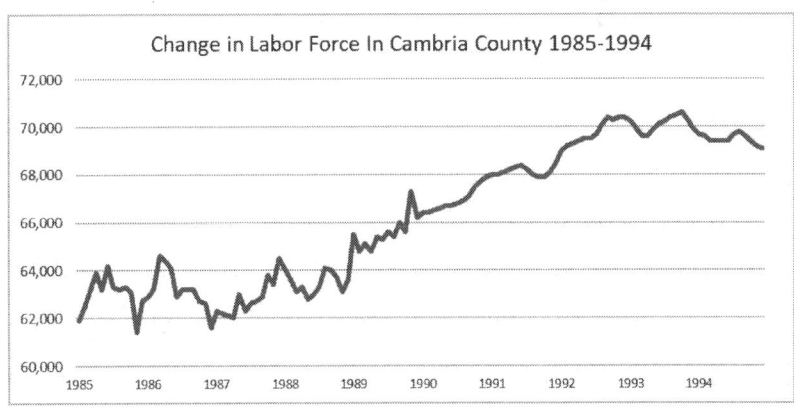

Figure 12b-Change in the Labor Force for Cambria County from 1985-1994 (Source: PA Department of Labor & Industry)

The population of Johnstown decreased from 35,496 in 1980 to 28,134, a 20.7% decline. During the same period the population of Cambria County decreased by 11.0% from 183,263 to 163,029. Of the county's decline, 36.4% of it occurred within the city limits of Johnstown. Congressman Murtha was able to bring some defense jobs to the area by placing the National Drug Intelligence center in the city and by enticing defense contractors to move to the area like the Concurrent Technologies Corporation.

V. JOHNSTOWN IN THE MID-90S TO POST-9/11

As the 20th century ended there was a period of relative calm. However there was an incident with the Anabaptists led by Bishop Ron McCrae teaming up with the KKK to drive a gay bar called the Casa Nova out of town (Pittsburgh Lesbian Correspondents, 2006; Levine, 2006). A complaint was filed with the Pennsylvania Human Relations Commission that kept the protesters off the bar's property, but they continued to protest across the street. The lack of business eventually forced the bar to close.

The new century brought the world's attention to the area when Flight 93 crashed into a field an hour away from the city in Shanksville. The plane was hijacked by four members of al-Qaida as a part of the 9/11 attacks. The hijackers were thwarted by the 40 passengers and crew on the plane. No one on the ground was killed.

The next year world attention was focused on the area with the Quecreek mine accident. Nine coal miners were trapped underground for 3 days. All miners were rescued (Pittsburgh Post-Gazette, 2002).

The motorcycle rally, Thunder in the Valley, came to the city in June 1998 and has been going there every June ever since. It now brings over 200,000 motorcyclists to Johnstown annually.

The Point Stadium was originally built in 1926 at the confluence of the Stonycreek and Little Conemaugh rivers right before the Stone Bridge. It seated 17,000 people. It had hosted many high school football games (many hosted by Bishop McCort and Johnstown High Schools), AAABA tournaments, and concerts. During the 1987 NFL players strike, the Pittsburgh Steelers practiced there with replacement players. After almost 80 years it was rusty and falling apart. In 2005 it was torn down and a 10,000-seat stadium was put in its place. The stadium was later named for Sargent's Personnel Agency, a temp agency.

1997 Economic Census

Table 2
Minority and Women Owned Businesses in Greater Johnstown 1997.

Group	All Firms			
	Firms (number)	% of firms	Sales and Receipts ($1,000)	% of sales
Universe (All Firms)	14,603		8,663,607	
Total minorities	270	1.8	80,460	0.9
Women	3259	22.3	447,949	5.2
Male White	11,074	75.8	8,135,198	93.9

Source 1997 economic census
https://www.census.gov/epcd/mwb97/metro/M3680.html

In 1997 the Census Bureau surveyed businesses owned minority and women owned businesses in Greater Johnstown (including Somerset and Cambria counties). The census bureau defines a firm as

"A business organization or entity consisting of one domestic establishment (location) or more under common ownership or control. All establishments of subsidiary firms are included as part of the owning or controlling firm. For the economic census, the terms "firm" and "company" are synonymous (Census Bureau)."

Only 1.8% of businesses in the economic census were minority owned and accounted for 0.9% of sales. The 22.3% of businesses owned by women only accounted for 5.2% of sales. White male-owned businesses accounted for 75.8% of all firms and 93.9% of all sales. When the total sales are divided by the total number of firms, the minority firms received $298,000 per firm, women owned businesses received $137,450 per firm and white male owned businesses received $734,621 per firm.

Appendix A shows the distribution of women owned firms by industry category. Slightly over half (50.9%) of the women owned businesses were service industries while they only made up 36.4% of all businesses. Retail trade accounted for the highest percentage of receipts, 33.9% in women owned businesses, while consisting of 21.7% of all businesses. As a percentage of the industry group, women owned businesses made up of the highest percentage of service industries at 36.4%. In terms of sales per firm, women owned construction industries, sub-dividers, and developers outperformed the overall category at $295 per firm compared to $218 per firm. Subsequent economic censuses were limited to Cambria County and did not look at minority and women owned businesses.

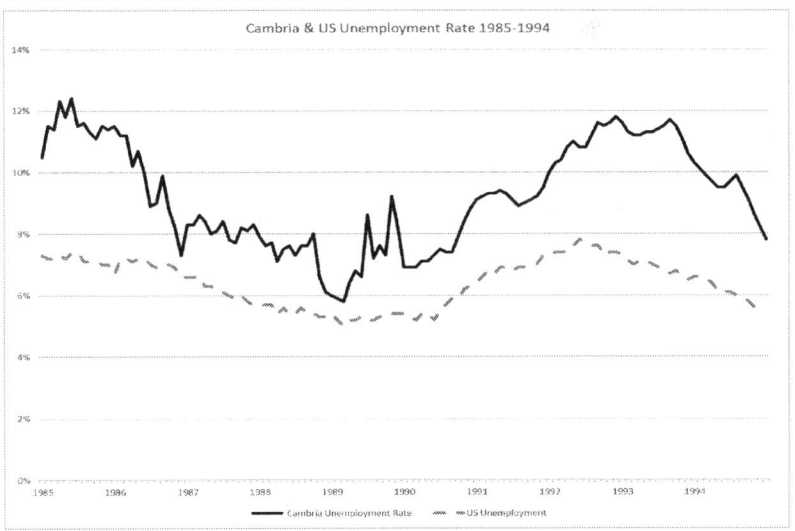

Figure 13a, Change in the Unemployment rate from 1995 to 2004 (Source: PA Department of Labor & Industry)

The unemployment rate decreased in the late '90s in Cambria County to under 5.5% and then increased to just under 7% in 2004, as can be seen in Figure 13a. The change in the rate was accompanied by the shrinking size of the labor force from 70,000 to 67,000 (Figure 13b). From 1990 to 2000 the city's population shrank from 28,134 to 23,906, a decrease of an additional 15%. The surrounding county had a decrease of 6.4% over the same period from 163,029 to 152,598.

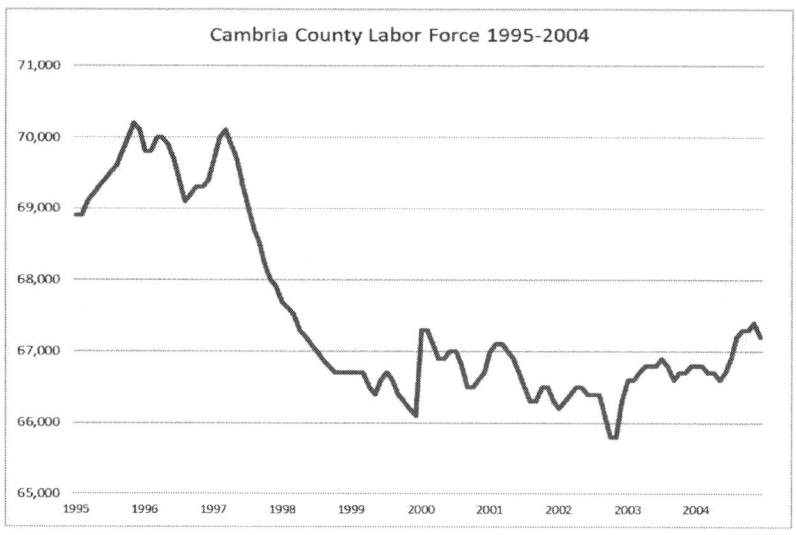

Figure 13b, The change in the workforce (Source: PA Department of Labor & Industry)

VI. THE GREAT RECESSION AND BEYOND

The last half of the first decade of the third millennium brought further economic anxiety to the area. The National Drug Intelligence Center was moved out of the area after Congressman John Murtha died. The population of the city decreased by an additional 12.2% from 2000 to 2010 to 20,978. The unemployment rate peaked at 10% in February 2010. During this period, the unemployment rate for the county mirrored that of the rest of the U.S. (Figure 14a). However further decreases in the unemployment rate are attributable to the decrease in the labor force as seen in Figure 14b. There was a sharp decline in the labor force in 2010.

During this period, hydraulic fracturing or fracking became a common method of obtaining natural gas from the Marcellus Shale rock formation throughout the Pennsylvania and New York state. The method involves fracturing the shale rock with a brine of chemicals. As a result, the natural gas bubbles up out of the shale like bubbles in soda. Families are paid a certain amount of money for having gas wells on their property and must sign nondisclosure agreements in return.

In 2015, Johnstown, PA was named the first Hockeyville USA in an online contest run by Kraft Foods. This was due to its history with the movie Slap Shot and to its long history of pro, semi pro, and amateur hockey in the U.S. After the Johnstown Chiefs left town in 2010, the city recruited an elite amateur team called the Johnstown Tomahawks in 2012.

Figure 14a, Unemployment rate in Cambria (solid line) and the U.S (dotted line) from 2005-2014 (Source: PA Department of Labor & Industry).

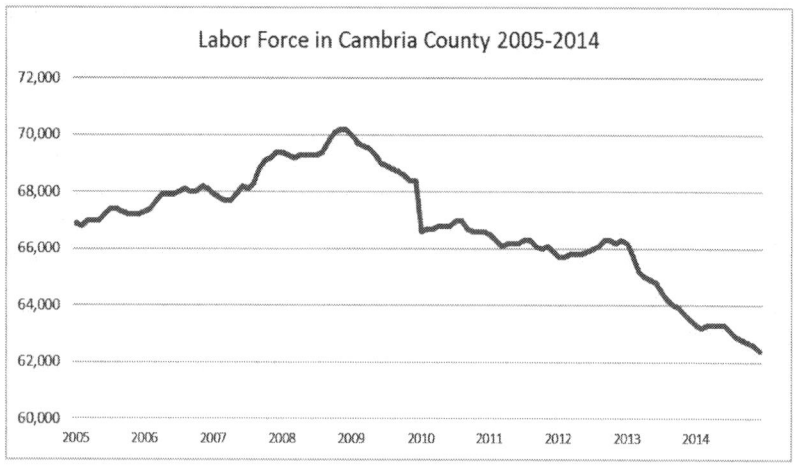

Figure 14b, The change in the labor force in Cambria County from 2005-(Source: PA Department of Labor & Industry)

City and County Demographics in 2010

Eighty percent of the city's 20,978 inhabitants were Caucasian in the 2010 census. For other racial/ethnic groups,14.6% were African American which is nearly a threefold increase in the city since 1960, 3.1% were Hispanic or Latino. The ethnic origins of the city were 22.3% German, 15.8% Irish, 12.9% Italian, 7.7% Slovak, and 6.7%, Polish. The median age of the city residents was 41.8 years. This means that half of the city residents were above 41.8 years of age and the other half were below. The U.S population median age in 2010 was 37.2 years.

At the same time, Cambria County was 95.8% white, 2.83% African American, and 0.89% Hispanic or Latino. The county median age was slightly lower than Johnstown's at 41 years.

Economic Census

The economic censuses of Johnstown Metropolitan Statistical Area (MSA) of 2002, 2007 and 2012 (which covered Cambria County), and Pennsylvania as a whole showed that there was an increase in the number of firms from 2002 to 2007 for the state, and for Cambria County. This increase corresponds to the increase in the labor force seen in Figure 14b. The increase leveled off by 2012 when the great recession hit and is presented in Figure 15a.

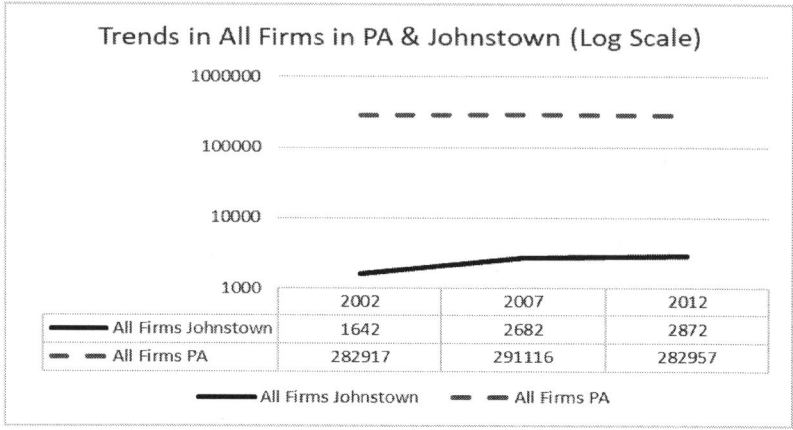

Figure 15a, Economic Census of the Johnstown Metropolitan Statistical Area and Pennsylvania as a whole (Source: Census Bureau)

Figure 15b shows three basic sectors listed in all three recent censuses: Retail, Wholesale Trade, and Manufacturing. These sectors did show a decrease of 8.5% in retail, 15.9% in manufacturing, and a 1.5% decrease in wholesale trade.

Figure 15b, Trend in selected business sectors listed in all three censuses (Source: Census Bureau).

Presidential Elections in Cambria County

From 1960 to 2000, Cambria County voted for the Democratic Presidential candidate in each presidential election. In 2004 George W. Bush won the county by 50.8% to 48.7% becoming the first Republican candidate to do so since Eisenhower in 1956. In 2008 Barack Obama won the county with 49.4% to 48.7% of the vote for John McCain. In 2008, the Democrats had 57,000 registered voters or 61.65% of the total registered. Republicans had 28,285 registrants or 30.59% of the total. Independents or third parties had 7,171 registrants or 7.76% of the total. This would change as the population of the county changed.

After Congressman Murtha died, his district was gerrymandered to stretch from Johnstown westward to the Ohio state line assuring that Republican Keith Rothfus was elected to his seat. Johnstown had a long tradition of electing Republican mayors. Linda Weaver, its first woman mayor, served one term in the 1990s and former school Greater Johnstown School District superintendent Donato Zucco was elected to two terms in the 2000s. After Donato Zucco served as mayor, the city changed the format of its government to a weak mayor system. Under this system the mayor is a glorified city council member with a city manager handling the day to day running of city services.

Act 47 Exit Plan

The city has been in Act 47 protection since 1992 for financially distressed municipalities. The Pennsylvania Department of Community and Economic Development issued a report detailing the city's progress under the law (Grass, 2018). There are 16 municipalities in Pennsylvania with this protection. Here is a summary.

The report states that one of the difficulties that the city has preventing it from leaving Act 47 is the lack of stability in the city leadership (Grass, 2018). Since 2008, the city has had six new members on council, seven city managers, and six finance directors. The turnover in city managers is due to City Council embers Jack Williams and Charlene Stanton flooding his or her office with many complaints and continuously introducing resolutions calling for their dismissal (Sutor, 2019c).

Even though the city's labor force had shrunk, the city had to increase its real estate tax from 36.44 mills in 2002 to 52.48 mills in 2010 under Act 47 (Grass, 2018). This increased the city's total revenue from this tax from $5,561,567 in 2002 to $6,560,262 in 2017. The amount collected per mill was $152,623 in 2002, but decreased to $125,005 in in 2017. Real estate taxes accounted for 39% of the city's revenue in 2017 (Grass, 2018).

The total value of the assessed property in the city was $263,735,070 in 1997 and $237,770,850 in 2017 (Grass, 2018). This decrease is due to a decline in nontaxable property values in the city from $119,033,130 in 1997 to $86,176,480 in 2017 (Grass, 2018).

Act 511 taxes account for 38% of the city's revenue bringing in $6,660,853 in 2017, a 20.38% increase from 2016 (Grass, 2018). These taxes are amusement taxes ($35,317), parking lot fees ($49,181), deed transfer fees ($68,789), local services taxes ($1,344,535), earned income taxes ($1,691,634), and business privilege taxes ($3,300,353) (Grass, 2018). The earned income revenue decreased in 2016 by 17.06% and in 2017 by an additional 4.86%. Business privilege taxes increased by 663% from 2016 to 2017. Local service taxes increased by 16% in 2017 (Grass, 2018).

In 2017 the police department accounted for 33% of expenditures in 2017 from the city's general fund. The fire department was second in expenditures at 29%, followed by public works at 15%. Police and fire department expenditures have increased in recent years while public works have decreased since 2015 (Grass, 2018).

The city had 134 full time employees in 2017, which is a 15% decrease from 2010 (Grass, 2018). Since 2013, the sewage department had the largest decrease in employees losing 20. The fire department lost seven employees. Only the police and the public works departments had a net gain in employees with three in each. Crime statistics are discussed later in this book. Further reductions in employees are expected in the future. The city received a federal grant to hire three additional police officers. Three employees from the sewage department were transferred to the public works department (Grass, 2018).

The city has 393 retirees to whom they have to pay a pension (Grass, 2018). The city's pension fund had $26,285,076 in assets in 2017, an 18% increase since 2013. The total liability for all pension funds for the city in 2017 was $49,662,193, leaving it 53% funded (Grass, 2018).

The New Sewer Line in Johnstown

The state mandated that the sewer system in Johnstown and surrounding communities be modernized by 2022 (Sutor, 2018). The Johnstown Redevelopment Authority operates the regional sewage system covering 20 municipalities. Old sewer lines had to be dug up and residents were required to pay for their homes to be connected to the line. The sewer line connections must pass a pressure test by the city. Depending on the size and age of the house, the cost for having it connected can easily run into the thousands of dollars. The Act 47 progress report listed the sewage system as the city's most valuable asset (Grass, 2018, p11).

Seventeen sewage systems serving 20 municipalities including Johnstown are connected to the Dornick Point sewage treatment plant. As of July 2019, there were 9,076 structures (buildings, homes, etc.) in the city limits that needed to be hooked up to the new sewer line. Of these, 3,439 structures had been pressure tested or 37.89% of the total in the city. Overall 56.72% of the 25.802 structures' sewer lines in the 20 municipalities have been pressure tested. East Conemaugh and Daisytown have had 100% of their structures tested while Southmont Boro (0.61%), West Taylor Township (1.26%), and Lorain Boro (17.43%) have had the lowest percentage of their structures pressure tested (Sutor, 2019d).

Fracking in Cambria County

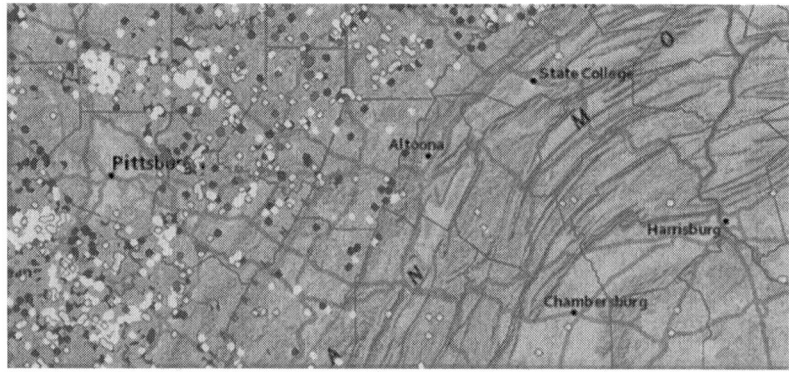

Figure 16, Unconventional Gas Wells in Southwestern PA in 2014 (Mapped/provided by FracTracker Alliance on FracTracker.org)

The film GasLand (Fox, 2010) written and directed by Josh Fox has raised awareness about the impact of hydraulic fracturing or fracking on the environment. The website FracTracker (2019) tracks the number of unconventional gas wells and the environmental violations that the state Department of Environmental Protection (DEP) cites. In 2014 the county had seven wells and seven violations. Looking at the current map that Fractracker has (Figure 18), I counted 17 wells in the county. Five of them have at least one DEP violation. These are colored white on the map above.

There are considerably more gas wells in neighboring counties to the west of Cambria, with a lot of wells with violations in Fayette, Westmoreland, Indiana and Washington counties. In the next chapter, the poor air quality in the county will be discussed. Is it due to the number of gas wells with violations which are upwind from Cambria County?

In a 2017 article, Fractracker found that the DEP received 43 complaints about wells in Cambria County. Twenty of these were complaints about water quality. The rest were complaints from municipalities. The most complaints were in Washington County.

Changes in the Parochial School System

Bishop McCort High School (my alma mater) and the other Catholic High Schools in the Altoona-Johnstown Diocese were transferred from its control under the Bishop (then Joseph Adamec) to an independent 501(c3) corporation in 2008. The corporation is now run by a Board of Trustees with the Bishop (now Mark Bartchak) included. According to their website, its tuition is now $6,550 per year. When I attended in the 1980s it was around $900. By comparison, Central Catholic

High School in Pittsburgh's annual tuition is $12,300 per year. When I attended, the school had over 600 students; now it has around 400. In 2013 the school started bringing in exchange students from China to fill the void of caused by decreasing enrollment. According to the website Guidestar (2019), McCort has $5,284,895 in gross receipts and $6,448,971 in assets in 2016.

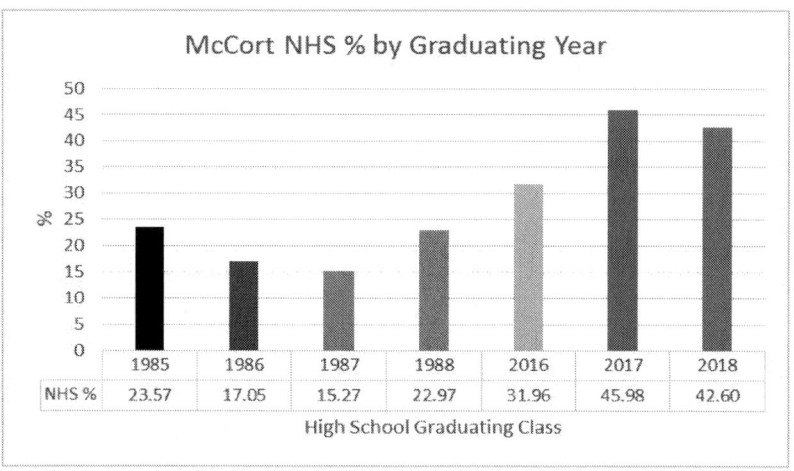

Figure 17, Percentage of Graduating Class in the National Honor Society at Bishop McCort High School (Source: Alumni News Letter, High School Yearbooks and the 1988 graduation program)

Looking at the published lists of the graduating classes at McCort, I noticed that there was a high percentage of students in the National Honor Society (NHS) in recent graduating classes. I went back and looked at the graduating classes from when I was there in the 1980s for comparison. The graph in Figure 17 shows that the percentage of graduating seniors for 2016, 2017, and 2018 were considerably higher than they were for classes in the '80s.

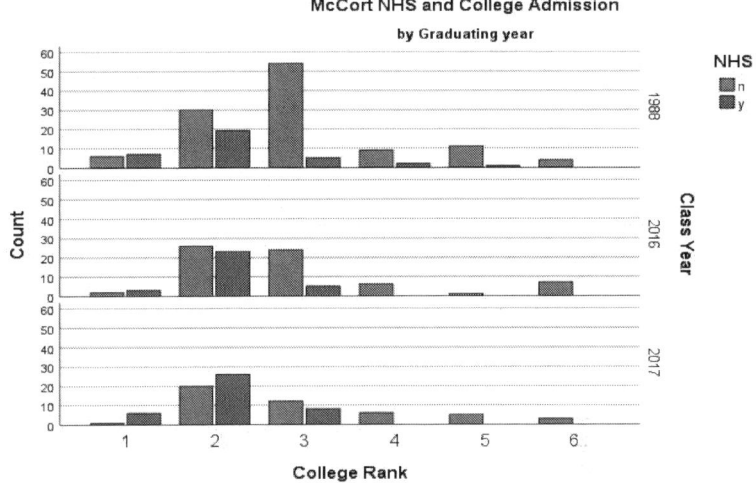

Figure 18, NHS and College Prestige Rank at Bishop McCort HS for 1988, 2016, and 2017. The 'n' refers to students not in the NHS and 'y' refers to those who are. (Source: Alumni News Letter, High School Yearbooks and the 1988 graduation program).

In Appendix B there is a table showing NHS membership in the McCort senior classes of 1988 (my graduating year), 2016, and 2017 and the prestige of college admissions as determined by U.S. News & World Report's College Admissions Rankings. An elite college had a score of 61-100 (for example, University of Pennsylvania, Johns-Hopkins), a second tier school had a score of 35-60 (University of Pittsburgh, Penn State University), a third tier four year school had a score of 34 or below or were unranked (Indiana University of Pennsylvania or IUP as we in PA call it). Community colleges, junior colleges, or advanced technical schools were fourth tier. Those who went into the military or were employed were placed in the fifth tier and those who were undecided or deferred for a year were placed in tier six. The classification for tier four, five, and six are totally mine and you are welcome to disagree with it. A logistic regression analysis showed that school year was not a predictor in prestige of college admissions, but NHS membership was regardless of school year. The numbers for the school year and the tier of college admission are summarized in Appendix B. The numbers in the Appendix B are summarized in Figure 18.

In 2020, a student from McCort won a full scholarship to the University of Pennsylvania (WJAC, 2020). It was a major media event in town.

After 2000, McCort was rattled by two scandals. The first involved Deacon and computer science teacher Thomas Lemmon, who had a relationship with a 15-year-old female student in 2003. He was then suspended by the Diocese and took the student to Canada. As the Canadian Police were bearing down on him he jumped to his death (Associated Press, 2003).

The second scandal involved Brother Stephen Baker who worked at McCort from 1992 to 2001 as an athletic trainer. Eighty-eight students were reportedly molested by him at McCort (Daily Caller, 2014). There were many others in other schools around the country molested by him. Brother Baker committed suicide in 2013. Principal Ken Salem and teacher Carol Grove were fired as a result. Many claim that Principal Salem did not know what Baker was doing. Because of these and other scandals, the state Attorney General launched a grand jury investigation of the Diocese.

The parochial elementary schools also underwent a restructuring. Greater Johnstown once had seven K through 8 Catholic schools. Gradually these schools were closed, and they were consolidated into the Divine Mercy Catholic Academy. The elementary students go to the former St. Benedict's School and the former Our Mother of Sorrows School. The middle school students go to the old Bishop McCort High School building where the freshmen and the sophomores used to have home rooms.

Healthcare Changes in Johnstown

In the '70s and '80s Johnstown, there were three main Hospitals: Lee, Mercy, and Memorial. Mercy was owned by the sisters of Mercy in 1911, Conemaugh Memorial and Lee Hospitals were public. Memorial Hospital was founded in 1889. Lee Hospital was founded in 1916 as a homeopathic hospital (Whittle, 2005, p. 69). In the 1990s, Mercy Hospital became Good Samaritan and Lee Hospital was bought up by the University of Pittsburgh Medical Center or UPMC. Later Conemaugh Memorial Hospital bought up Lee and Memorial hospital. In 2014, Conemaugh was bought up by the Duke LifePoint health care system as a for profit hospital. When this happened, the city could collect real estate taxes from the hospital (Grass, 2018).

VII. SEEING JOHNSTOWN THROUGH NEW EYES-COUNTY HEALTH RANKINGS

I was born in Johnstown in 1970. After finishing school, I had left town to live in Pittsburgh. Finances forced me to move back to the city in 2016. I was shocked to see how it had changed, with lots of abandoned houses and stories of the opioid crisis. As can be seen in Figure 19a, unemployment was still higher than the U.S. rate but decreasing. Figure 19b shows how the decrease in the rate for the county is due to shrinkage in the labor force.

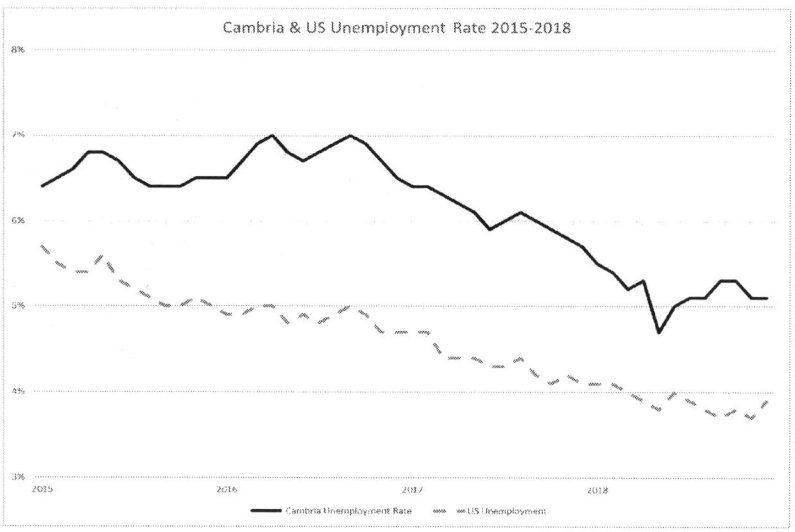

Figure 19a, Cambria & U.S Unemployment Rates 2015-2018 (Source: PA Department of Labor & Industry)

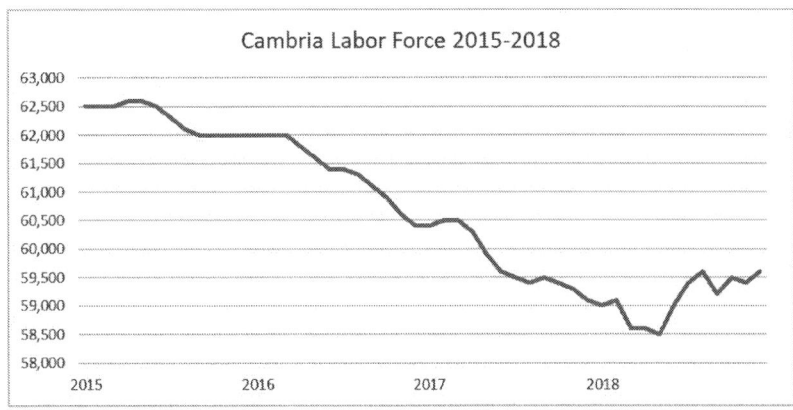

Figure 19b, Change in Cambria Labor Force from 2015-2018 (Source: PA Department of Labor & Industry)

County Health Rankings

According to the website County Health Rankings, in 2020 Cambria County ranked 64th out of 67 counties in Pennsylvania in health outcomes and 44th in health factors. Health outcomes are the length of life and quality of life factors described below. Health factors are variables that contribute to health outcomes such as health behaviors and clinical care.

In 2017 Cambria's rankings were 63rd for health outcomes and 43rd for health factors. In 2018, Cambria was 64th in health outcomes and 59th in health factors. In 2019, Cambria was ranked 65th in health outcomes and 56th in health factors. Philadelphia County ranked last on both measures in 2020. Union County ranked first on outcomes and Montgomery County was first on health factors in 2020.

While these composite rankings can generate headlines, it is more informative to look at the individual health measures that make up these rankings. There are 34 individual statistics that determined these rankings for 2020. Cambria's sub-rankings on health outcomes were 66th in Pennsylvania in length of life and 59th in quality of life. For health factors, the county ranked 25th in health behaviors, 50th in clinical care, 53rd in social and economic factors, and 57th in physical environment. These sub rankings are themselves composite measures of 34 specific health variables.

Length of Life and the Opioid Crisis

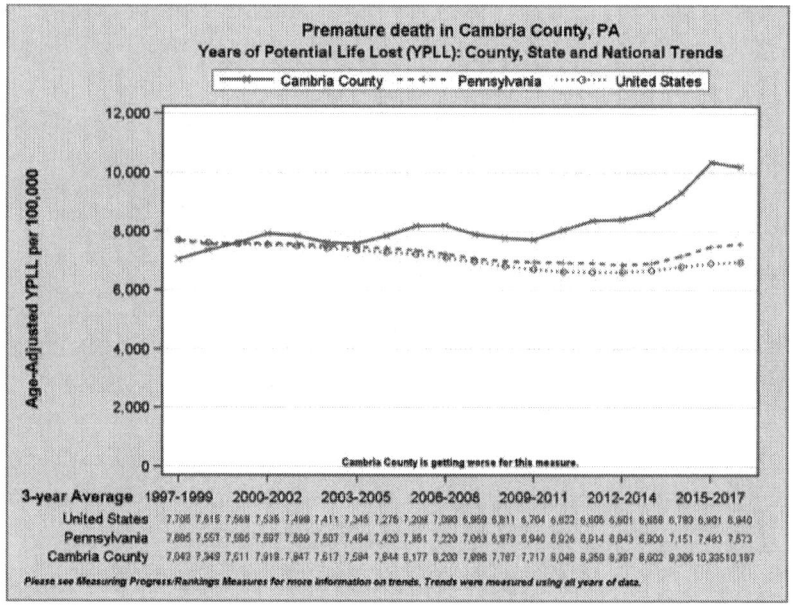

Figure 20, The Overall YPLL Rate for Cambria County vs. the United States and Pennsylvania from 1997-2017 (Source County Health Rankings)

Cambria County ranked 66th in years of potential life lost (YPLL) from the county with the lowest rate before age 75 with 10,187 years in the county lost per 100,000 people. For example, if someone dies at age 25, they have 50 YPLLs. It was 22,511 years per 100,000 people for African Americans which was the highest in the state by far. The second highest county in the state for African Americans was Fayette County at 15,131 years per 100,000. It was 9,689 years per 100,000 people for Caucasians in Cambria County which was the fourth highest in the state. For comparison, the rate was 7,573 years per 100,000 people in Pennsylvania and 6,900 years per 100,000 people in the U.S. YPLL and mortality determine the length of life ranking.

Life expectancy (the average age one is predicted to live at birth) was not included in the ranking for length of life but it is still illuminating. For Cambria County it is 75.8 years for 2016-2018 which is 2.5 years below the state rate of 78.3 years and 3 years below the U.S rate of 78.6 years. Overall, the county ranked 64th out of 67 counties in the state on this measure.

Life expectancy by race is summarized in Table 3. African Americans fared poorly in the county (65.6 years, the lowest in the state) relative to African Americans in the state (73.4 years) and the U.S. (74.8 years). Fifty-nine percent of African Americans in the county live within Johnstown's city limits. Eight children were homicide victims in Johnstown in 2017 (Sutor, 2017). Hispanics in the county have longer life expectancies (89.0 years, the 9th highest in the state) than African Americans or Caucasians (76.2 years, the 40th highest in the state), but Hispanics are 1.6% of the county population. Nationwide, Hispanics have longer life expectancies (81.8 years) than Caucasians (78.5 years) or African Americans (75.3 years).

Table 3
Life Expectancy in years in Cambria County, Pennsylvania and the U.S. in 2017 (Source National Center for Health Statistics - Mortality Files)

Group	Cambria County	Pennsylvania	U.S.
Overall	75.6	78.3	78.6
Caucasian	76.2	78.9*	78.8
African American	65.6	73.4*	75.3
Hispanic	89.0	85.3*	81.8

Pennsylvania life expectancy by race numbers are from 2010 (Measure of America, 2013)

The premature age adjusted mortality rate is the number of deaths among residents under age 75 per 100,000 which controls for age. For Cambria County the overall rate was 455 per 100,000 which was the 4th highest rate in the state for 2016-2018. The overall state rate was 359 per 100,000. The US rate is not available for this period. For African Americans, the county rate was 878 per 100,000 which was the second highest in the state. Neighboring Somerset County was the highest in the state at 958 per 100,000 for African Americans. For Caucasians, the rate was slightly more than half that of African Americans at 443 per 100,000 for this period which was third highest in the state.

Table 4
Years of Potential Life Lost (YPLL), Premature Age Adjusted Mortality, and Child Mortality Rates for Cambria County for periods where data was available (Source County Health Rankings)

	Period			
Cambria County YPLL Rate	2012-2014	2014-2016	2015-2017	2016-2018
Overall	8,397	8,602	10,335	10,187
Caucasian		8,424	9,671	9,689
African American		14,892	24,443	22,511
Age Adjusted Mortality	2013-2015	2014-2016	2015-2017	2016-2018
Overall	410	435	463	455
Caucasian		422	448	443
African American		789	885	878
Child Mortality	2012-2015	2013-2016	2014-2017	2016-2018
Overall	52	56.7	60	51
Caucasian		48.3	43	37
African American		171.5	253	235

A clue to the reasons for the low life expectancy among African Americans in the county is provided by the rate of child mortality in the county. Child mortality is defined as the number of deaths among children under the age of 18 per 100,000 persons. The overall county rate was 51 deaths per 100,000 residents which was the 26th highest rate in the state. For African Americans, the rate was 235 per 100,000 residents which was by far the highest in the state. Only 20 counties reported child mortality rates for African Americans in Pennsylvania, 22 counties report for Caucasians, and 60 counties report overall rates. For Caucasians in the county, it was 37 per 100,000 residents, almost six times lower but ranked 12th in the state out of 22 counties reporting. The overall state rate for child mortality was 49 per

100,000 residents.

The recent trends in YPLL, in age adjusted mortality, premature age adjusted mortality, and in child mortality for the county are presented in Table 4 and Figure 21. County health data by race are only available after 2017. Only the most recent periods in which they were provided are listed in the table.

There does appear to be a spike in child mortality among African Americans in 2014-2017 which appears to be driving the low life expectancy numbers for the county. The three timepoints available by race suggest a consistent pattern among groups. The spate of eight homicides in the city in 2017 (Stanish, 2017) is part of what is driving the elevated child mortality numbers. However, the numbers from the previous period (2013-2016, 171.5 deaths per 100,000 people) were also elevated relative to Caucasian rates in the same period.

The infant mortality rate for the county was 6 per 1,000 live births which is the same as the state and US rates. It ranked 30th in the state. There are no county rankings or racial rates for this measure as not all of them report rates.

Much has been written about the opioid epidemic in the U.S. How does it relate to The University of Pittsburgh has a tracker web for the number of overdose deaths in each county in the Pennsylvania called OverdoseFreePA (2020). It lists 329 deaths in Cambria County from 2015 to 2019 (Figure 20). Of these 67% of the deaths were male and 90% of the deaths were Caucasian. At the same time, only 8% of the deaths were African American. The percentage of African American deaths in the county was lower than the percentage of African American overdose deaths statewide in 2017 (12%). This is higher than their percentage in the state population (10.8%). Caucasians accounted for 79% of the deaths statewide in 2017.

The 25-34-year-old age group accounted for the most deaths at 100, followed by the 35-44 age group at 88 and the 45-54 age group at 62. These age groups accounted for 76% of the overdose deaths in the county. One hundred eighty-one or 55% of the deaths had an undefined zip code. Of the remaining 148 with a defined zip code, 95 or 29% of the total were in Johnstown and/or Greater Johnstown.

The most common drug found in the deceased over this period was fentanyl (194 cases or 59%). The second most common was heroin at 109 or 33.1% followed by cocaine at 63 or 19.1%, oxycodone at 49 or 14.9%, and alprazolam at 48 or 14.6%. Of the top five drugs, three (fentanyl, heroin, and oxycodone) are opioids, cocaine is a stimulant, and alprazolam is an addictive anti-anxiety medication. The report does not state how many of the deaths had more than one drug in their system.

The breakdown of deaths by age and race were not available at the county level in the report but statewide in 2017, Caucasians age 25-34 account for 39% of the deaths for their group which is the largest percentage. For African Americans, the percentage is roughly equal for the age groups between 25 and 64 (OverdoseFreePA, 2020).

Table 5
Population adjusted Drug Overdose Deaths in Cambria County and Surrounding Counties

County	Deaths 2015-2018	2018 Population	Deaths/100,000
Cambria	299	131,730	227
Bedford	41	48,176	85.1
Blair	141	122,492	115.1
Centre	72	162,805	44.2
Clearfield	52	79,388	65.5
Fayette	219	130,441	167.9
Indiana	157	84,501	185.8
Somerset	98	73,952	132.5
Philadelphia	3,960	1,584,138	250.0
Allegheny	2,251	1,218,452	209.4
Pennsylvania	17,900	12,807,060	139.8

Table 5 shows the population adjusted overdose deaths from 2015-2018 for Cambria and surrounding counties of Bedford, Blair, Centre, Clearfield, Fayette, Indiana, and Somerset. At 227 deaths per 100,000 residents, Cambria County had the highest death rate in the area, followed by Indiana at 185.5 deaths per 100,000 people. When comparing Cambria to the most populous counties in the state, Philadelphia County had a higher rate at 250 deaths per 100,000 persons while Allegheny County, which includes Pittsburgh, was lower at 184.1 deaths per 100,000 persons. A Drug Enforcement Administration (DEA, 2018) report does show that the rate for Cambria County was the second highest for the state in 2016 and the third highest in 2017. County rankings for 2018 were not available in the report. The state rate for this period was abstracted from the DEA report and from a report from the Johnstown Tribune-Democrat (Finnerty, 2019). The state rate was 139.8 deaths per 100,000 persons for this period.

In 2019, the Cambria County Coroner, Jeff Lees reported that the number of drug overdoses decreased to 30. Other counties and the state overall have not reported their 2019 numbers to OverdoseFreePA, so they are not represented in Table 5. The trend in drug overdoses is shown in Figure 21.

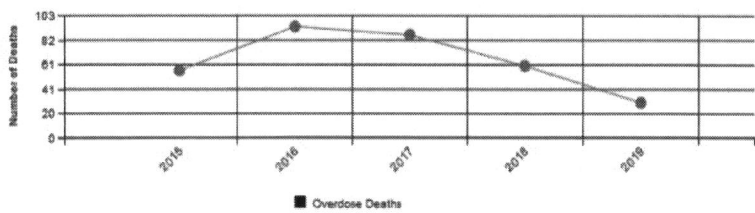

Figure 21, Drug overdose deaths by year for Cambria County 2015-2019

Individual County Health Measures

The trend charts for Figure 20 and for Figures 22 through 34 comparing the county, the state, and the U.S. were provided by County Health Rankings for comparison for certain measures for the county, state, and the U.S. County Health Rankings made the determination of whether the county was improving on a given measure relative to past data. Only overall measures for the county are provided. The numbers are not broken down by individual demographics within the county in the charts but are provided in the bullets when available

Below is a list of the statistics driving the poor health outcome rankings for Cambria County. The sub-bullets are related statistics which were provided by County Health Rankings but were not factored into the rankings. The sub-bullet statistics are still illuminating in that they provide a valuable context for the overall rankings.

Quality of Life

The quality of life ranking of 59th for Cambria County is determined by these factors.

- Those who describe their health as fair or poor in Cambria County in 2017 was 17% which was 1% below the state average and the same as the national average of 16%. The county had a rank of 49th on this measure out of 67 counties in the state.
- People in the county describe having 4.6 days of poor physical health in the last 30 days in 2017, where the state rate was 4.4 days, and the U.S. rate was four days. This gives the county a ranking of 56th in the state on this measure.
  - An estimated 12% of adults in the county report "frequent physical distress" in 2017. This is the percentage of adults reporting 14 or more days of poor physical health per month. This is 1% lower than the state rate and is the same as the U.S. rate. The county ranked 48th in the state.
- People in the county reported an average of 4.2 poor mental health days in 2017, which was lower than the 4.3 days than the state reported, but more than the 3.8 average in the U.S giving the county a ranking of 55th on this measure.
  - An estimated 14% of adults in the county report "frequent mental distress" in 2017. Like frequent physical distress, this is the percentage of adults reporting 14 or more days of poor mental health per month. This rate is the same as the

state rate and 2% higher than the US rate. The county ranked 54th in the state.
- The last quality of life measure was the percentage of low birthweight (LBW) babies from 2012-2018. The county reported 9% LBW babies, which was higher than the state and U.S rates of 8%. African Americans in Cambria County reported 16% LBW babies, Hispanics had 10% LBW babies, and Caucasians had 8% LBW. This gives the county a ranking of 59th on this measure.

Health Factors Sub-measures

The factors determining the county's health behavior ranking of 25th are:
- Eighteen percent of adults in the county were smokers in 2017. This was 1% higher than the U.S rate, and 1% less than the state rate on this measure. This gives the county a rank of 36th in

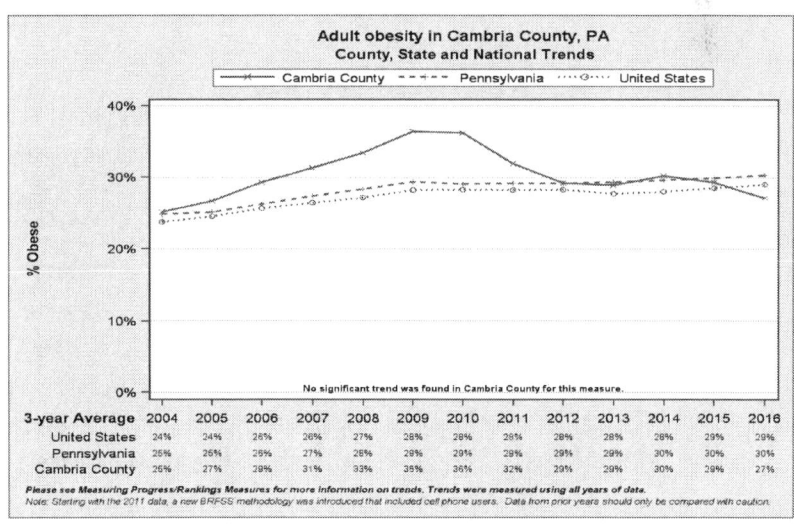

Figure 22, Trend in Adult Obesity from 2004-2015 for Cambria County, PA and U.S. (Source County Health Rankings)

the state.
- ○ The rate of drug overdose mortality in the county was 61 per 100,000 which placed it worst in the state, which had a rate of 38 per 100,000. This rate covers 2016-2018. The county had a rate of 63rd in the state.

- The adult obesity rate for the county was 27% in 2016 which was 3% lower than the state rate of 30% and 2% lower than the U.S rate giving a rank of 8th on this measure. The news isn't all bad. Figure 22 shows that there was a spike in obesity rates in 2009 and 2010, which was above the U.S and state rates. Afterward it lowered to below the state rate by 2016.
  - ○ However, the rate of adults with diabetes in 2016 (14%) is higher than the state and US rates of 11% putting it in a tie for 60th in the state.
- The food environment index measures factors that contribute to a healthy food environment with zero being worst and ten being the best. For Cambria County, the index of 7.5 from 2015 and 2017 was below the state rate of 8.2 and the U.S rate of 7.6 giving the county a rank of 61st on this measure.
  - ○ Thirteen percent of the county was food insecure in 2017 which was 1% higher than the state rate and 2% higher than the US rate. The county ranked 57th in the state from the lowest rate.
  - ○ Nine percent had limited access to healthy foods in 2015 which is higher than the state

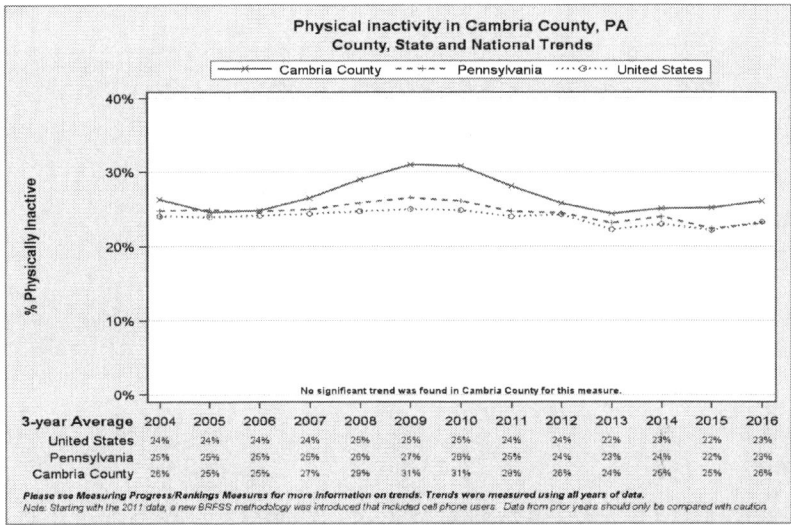

Figure 23, Trends in Physical Inactivity Rates for Cambria, PA, and U.S from 2004-2015 (Source County Health Rankings)

rate of 5% giving it a rank of 61st in the state.
- The physical inactivity rate of 26% in the county in 2016 was higher than the state rate of 22% and the U.S rate of 22%. This gives the county a rank of 39th on this measure in the state.
- The percent of those in the county with access to exercise opportunities in 2010 and 2019 (80%) was lower than the state rate of 84% and the U.S rate of 84%. This percentage did give the county a rank of 40th on this measure. This is defined as "percentage of persons with adequate access to locations for physical activities."
    ○ Thirty-six percent of adults in the county report insufficient sleep in 2016 (less than seven hours) which was 2% lower than the state rate but it was ranked 49th among the other counties.
- The percentage of those drinking excessively or binge drinking in the county in 2017 was 19% which was the same as the state rate and the U.S

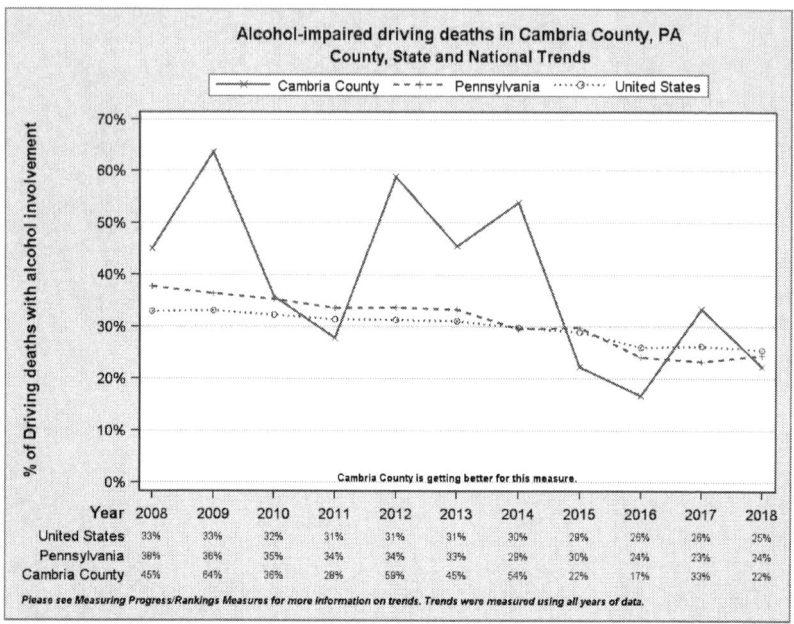

Figure 24, Percentage of Driving Deaths that are Alcohol Related in Cambria, PA, and U.S from 2008-2017 (Source County Health Rankings)

rate, giving it a rank of 14th on this measure from the county with the lowest rate.

- Thirty one percent of driving deaths were alcohol-related in the county which was higher than the state rate of 27% and the U.S rate of 28% for the years 2014-2018. The county ranked 46th in the state on this measure. Figure 24 shows that the trend in the percentage of these deaths fluctuates from year to year. Counties with larger populations would have more stable rates.
  - The motor vehicle crash death rate in the county was 11 per 100,000 from 2012-2018 which is higher than the state rate of 10 per 100,000 and the same as the U.S. rate but it ranked 42nd from the county with the lowest rate.

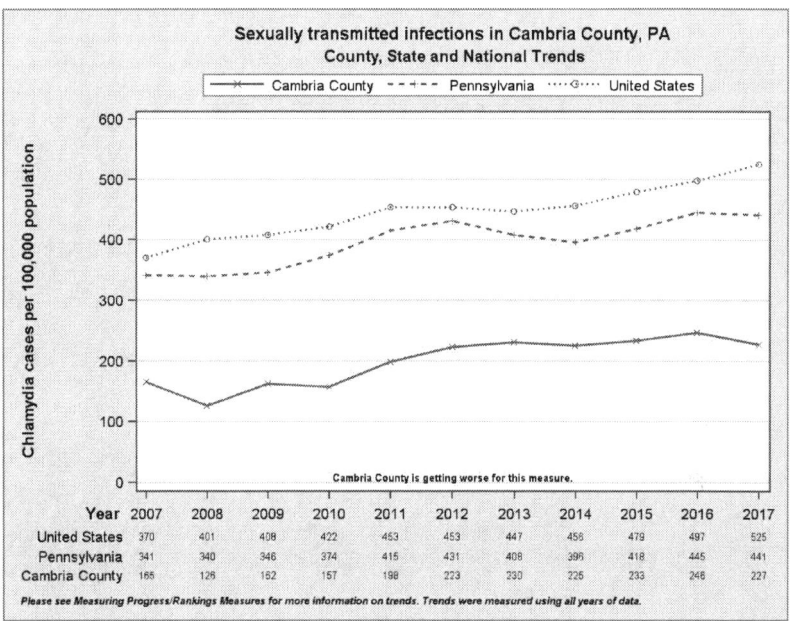

Figure 25, Sexually transmitted disease rates for Cambria, PA, and U.S from 2007 to 2016 (Source County Health Rankings)

- The rate of chlamydia was 227 cases per 100,000 in 2017 which was lower than the state rate of 440.8 cases per 100,000 and the U.S rate of 524.6 cases per 100,000 giving it a rank of 33rd in the state on this measure. Figure 25 shows that the STD rate in Cambria County has been consistently lower than the state and U.S rate. The rates for all three entities have been steadily rising.
  ○ There were no reports of HIV prevalence for any county in Pennsylvania in the 2020 release but in the 2019 release the rate was 105 per 100,000 for the county for 2015 which was lower than the state rate of 314 per 100,000. The U.S. rate was 341 per 100,000 residents in 2016 which was the most recent year available.

- The teen birth rate in the county was 21 births per 1,000 live births in the female population aged 15-19 from 2012-2018 which was higher than the state rate of 18 births per 1,000 but below the U.S rate of 23 births per 1,000. In the county it was 58 births per 1,000 for African Americans, 20 births/1000 for Hispanics and 19 per 1,000 for Caucasians. The county had a rank of 36th in the state on this measure.

The measures determining the clinical care ranking of 50th for the county were:

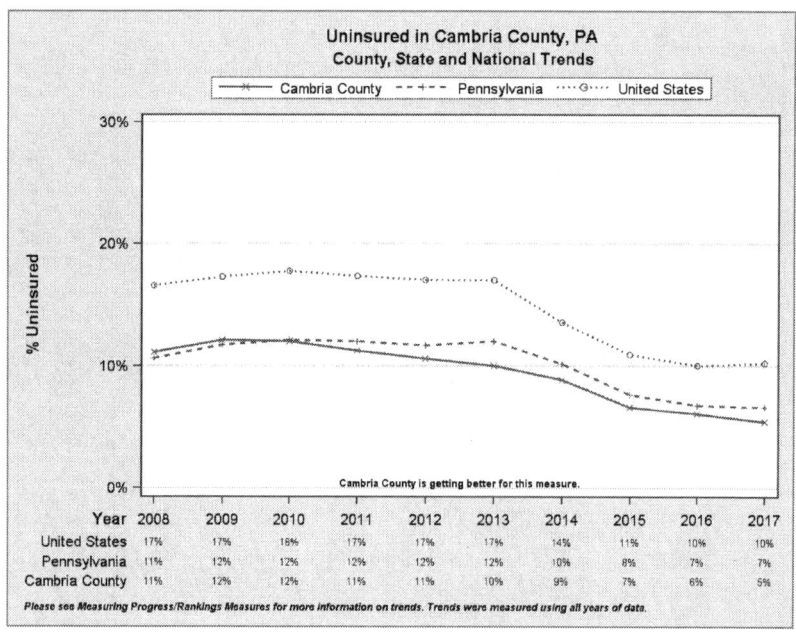

Figure 26, Trends in the Uninsured in Cambria, PA, and U.S from 2008 to 2016 (Source County Health Rankings)

- The county's uninsured rate of 5% for 2017 was lower than the state rate of 7% and the U.S rate of 10%. This could be partly due to Medicaid expansion under the Affordable Care Act. The county ranked 9th on this measure from the county with the lowest rate. Figure 26 shows that since 2011 the uninsured rate has fallen below the state and U.S rate.
  - Three percent of children in the county were uninsured for 2017 which was 1% lower than the state rate and 2% lower than the U.S. rate giving it a rank of 7th in the state.
  - Six percent of adults in the state were uninsured for 2017 which is 1% lower than the state rate and 8% lower than the U.S. rate. The county had a ranking of 10th in the state on this measure from the county with the lowest rate.

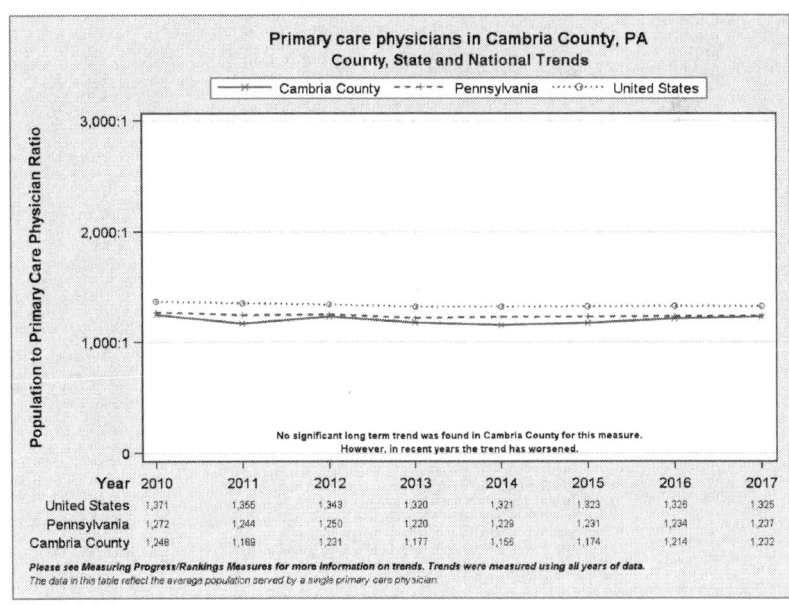

Figure 27, Ratio of primary care physicians to population for Cambria, PA, and U.S from 2010 to 2016 (Source County Health Rankings)

- The availability of primary care physicians (PCPs) for 2017 was slightly better (1232 persons for each physician), than in the state (1237 persons for each PCP), and in the U.S (1330 persons for each PCP) ranking 52nd in the state on this measure. Figure 27 shows that the trend for Cambria County is barely distinguishable from the state and U.S rates.
  ○ The rate of other primary care providers such as nurse practitioners was 712 persons per provider for 2019 which was lower than the state rate of 855 persons per provider. This gave the county a rank of 54th in the state from county with the highest rate.

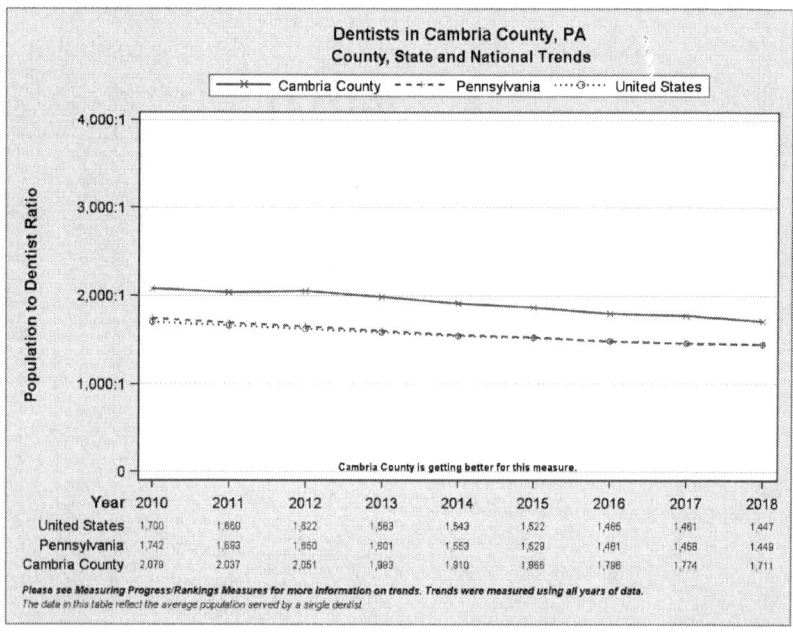

Figure 28, Ratio of dentists to population for Cambria, PA, and U.S from 2010 to 2017 (Source County Health Rankings)

- The ratio of persons per provider for dentists for 2018 was worse in Cambria County (1711 persons per dentist) than in the state (1,449 per dentist) and the U.S (1,450 per dentist) ranking 45th on this measure. Figure 28 shows some improvement for Cambria County in this ratio which could be due to population loss.
- The ratio of persons per mental health providers in 2019 was 509 persons per provider in Cambria County which was slightly worse than the state rate (484 persons per provider) and the U.S (440/provider) ranking 18th on this measure.

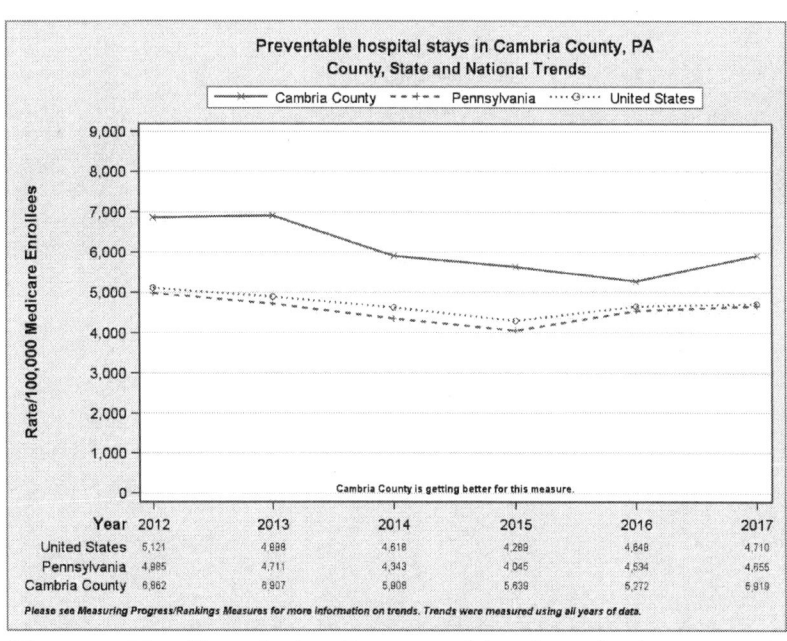

Figure 29, Trend in Preventable hospital stays in Cambria, PA, and U.S from 2012 to 2016 for Medicare enrollees (Source County Health Rankings)

- County Health Rankings defines preventable hospital status as "hospital stays for ambulatory care sensitive conditions... which can be treated in outpatient settings." The rate of preventable hospital stays was higher in the county in 2017 (5,919 stays per 100,000 Medicare enrollees) than in the state (4,655 stays per 100,000 enrollees) and the U.S. (4,535 stays per 100,000) (Figure 29). For African Americans, the rate was 6,653 stays per 100,000, for Hispanics it was 16,420 stays per 100,000, and for Caucasians it was 5,773 stays per 100,000. The county ranked 62nd in the state on this measure. Figure 29 shows some improvement on this measure for Cambria County for the overall rate.

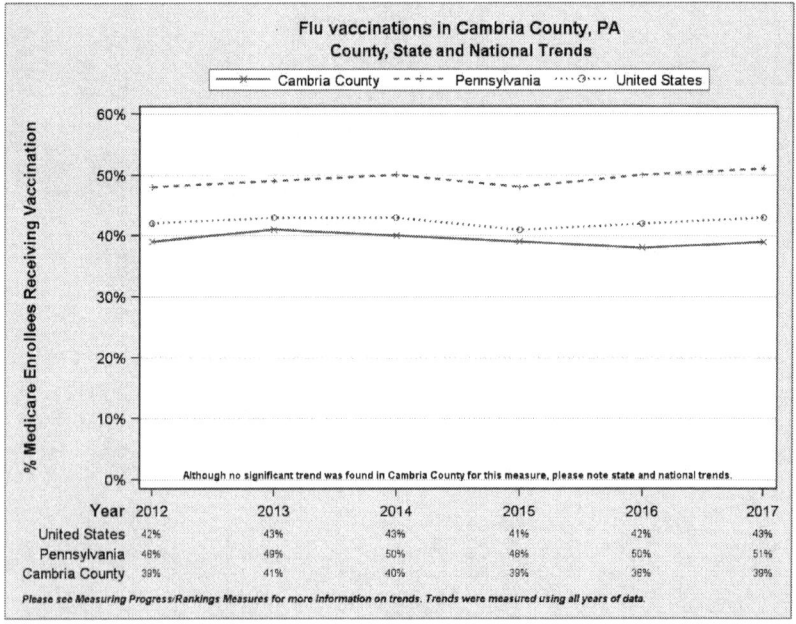

Figure 30, Flu vaccination rates for Cambria, PA, and U.S from 2012 to 2016 for Medicare enrollees (Source County Health Rankings)

- The county rate of those receiving flu vaccines in 2017 (37%) was lower than the state rate of 51% and the U.S rate of 46% (Figure 30). The African American rate in the county was 34%. The average was 38% for Asians, 46% for Hispanics, and 39% Caucasians. The county ranked 62nd in the state on this measure.

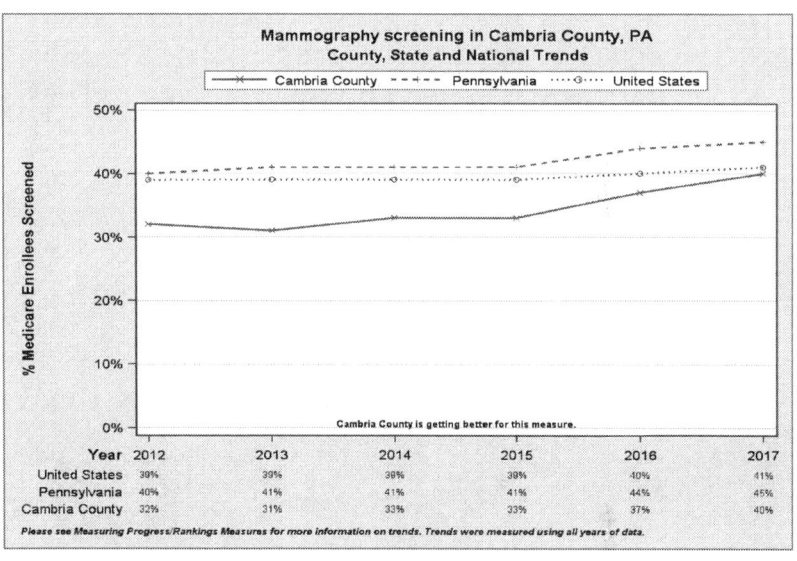

Figure 31, Mammography screening rates for Cambria, PA, and U.S from 2012 to 2016 for Medicare enrollees (Source County Health Rankings)

- The rate of mammography for female Medicare enrollees in 2017 was 40% in the county while it was 45% in PA and 42% in the U.S. For African Americans in the county it was 38%, for Hispanics it was 50%, and for Caucasians it was 40%. The county ranked 60th in the state on this measure. Figure 31 shows some improvement of mammography for the overall rate for the county. Like the flu vaccine data, this suggests racial disparities in preventive healthcare services for older residents of the county.

The factors influencing the county's social and economic environment rank of 53rd in the state are:
- The high school graduation rate of 93% in the county for 2016-2017 was better than the state rate of 87% and the U.S rate of 85%. The county ranked 9th in the state on this measure.
- Sixty two percent in the of adults age 25-44 in the county from 2014-2018 have had some college at some point in their lives which was slightly less than the state rate of 65% and the U.S rate of 66%. The county ranked 18th in the state on this measure.

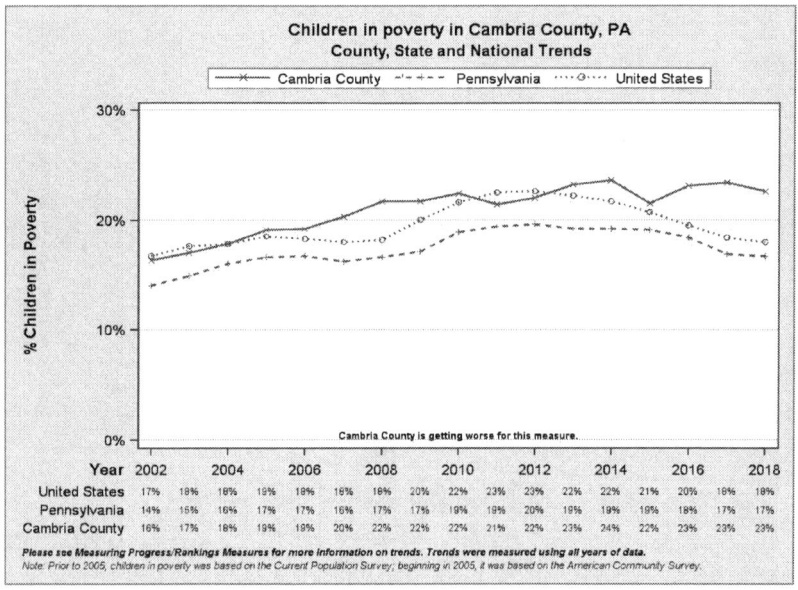

Figure 32, Trends in child poverty for Cambria, PA, & U.S from 2002 to 2018 (Source County Health Rankings)

- Twenty three percent of children in the county were below the poverty level in 2018 (Figure 32). In the state the rate was 17% and, in the U.S, it is 18%. For African Americans, the rate was 75%, for Hispanics it was 63%, and for Caucasians it was 20%. The county ranked 11th overall on

this measure.
- ○ The median household income for African Americans in the county in 2018 was $17,687, for Hispanics it was $35,574, and for Caucasians $45,940. Overall, it was $47,228 for the county giving a rank of 64th from the highest income in the state. For the state $60,891 and for the U.S. it was $60,293.
- ○ Fifty-two percent of children in the county qualify for free or reduced cost lunch from 2017-2018 which is 2% higher than the state rate. The county ranked 50th from the highest county percentage.
- The ratio of income inequality from 2014-2018 (the ratio of the 80th percentile income to the 20th percentile) was 4.7 in the county which was lower than the state rate of 4.8 and the U.S rate of 4.9. The county ranked 10th in the state on this measure. The statewide rate is skewed by the high rate in Philadelphia county of 6.2.
  - ○ The residential segregation index from 2014-2018 for African Americans vs. Caucasians for the county was 72 which was point higher than the state rate. The county was tied for 3rd from the highest index in the state. Higher values indicate greater African American/Caucasian separation in the county. There are many counties in the state with small minority populations and small segregation indexes.
  - ○ The residential segregation index for white vs. non-white residents from 2014-2018 for the county was 59 which was 1 point lower the state rate. Among the counties, it ranked 3rd from the highest value in the state. Higher values indicate greater non-white/white separation in the county. There are many

counties in the state with small minority populations and small segregation indexes. Three counties, Cameron, Forest, and Sullivan had no black/white or white/non-white segregation index values.
- The rate of children in single parent households from 2014-2018 was 2% higher in the county (36%) as it was in the state (34%) and the U.S (33%). The county ranked 11th on this measure.
- The rate of social association memberships per 10,000 was higher in the county in 2017 (20.1 per 10,000 in the population) than in the state (12.3 per 10,000) and in the U.S (9 per 10,000). The county ranked 6th in the state on this measure.
  ○ Five percent of youth in the county were socially disconnected from 2014-2018 which was 1% lower than the state rate giving it a rank of 14th from the county with the lowest rate.

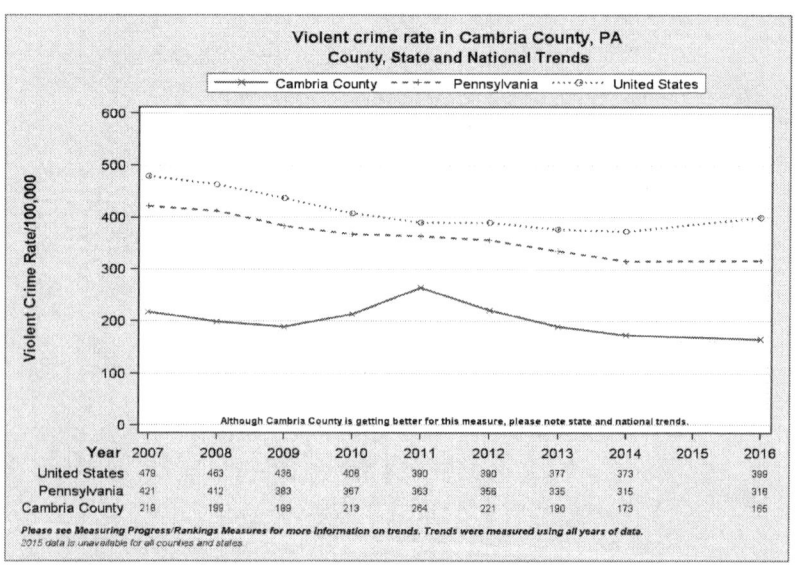

Figure 33, Violent Crime rate from Cambria, PA, and U.S from 2007 to 2016 (Source County Health Rankings)

- The violent crime rate in the county was 169 incidents per 100,000 residents from 2014-2016 which was lower than the state rate of 315 per 100,000 and the U.S rate of 386 per 100,000. The county ranked 38th or near the middle of PA counties on this measure. Figure 33 shows that the rate has decreased since 2011 for the county. This mirrors decreases in the state and the U.S. The violent crime rate for the city will be looked at in a later chapter.
  - The county homicide rate was 1% higher than state rate of five per 100,000 residents for 2012-2018. It was ranked 6th among the counties from the highest rate in the state (Philadelphia at 19 per 100,000). For African Americans the rate was 50 per 100,000 which was the highest in the state. For Caucasians it was 2 per 100,000.
  - The county suicide rate was 19 per 100,000 residents which was well above the state and U.S. rates of 14 per 100,000. The county ranked 15th in the state from the county with the highest rate on this measure.
  - The juvenile arrest rate of 18 per 100.000 residents was the same as the state rate. The county was tied for 30th in the state on this measure.
- The injury death rate was 123 per 100,000 persons in the county for 2014-2018 which was much higher than the state rate of 86 per 100,000 and 70 per 100,000 in the U.S. The county was first in the state on this measure. For African Americans the rate was 214 per 100,000 while for Caucasians it was 121 per 100,000.
  - The motor vehicle crash death rate was 11 per 100,000 residents in the county from 2012-

2018 giving it a rank of 42nd in the state from the county with the highest rate. This was above the state rate of 10 per 100,000 and was the same as the U.S. rate. For this measure, high population counties such as Philadelphia have low rates (7 per 100,00) while low population counties have high rates such as Bedford County (21 per 100,000).

○ The rate of firearm fatalities was 17 per 100,000 in the county was 2014-2018 which was higher than the state rate of 12 per 100,000. For African Americans in the county it was 60 per 100,000 and for Caucasians it was 16 per 100,000. The county was tied for 6th from the highest county rate in the state.

Physical Environment

The factors affecting the county's rank of 57th in the state on the physical environment are:

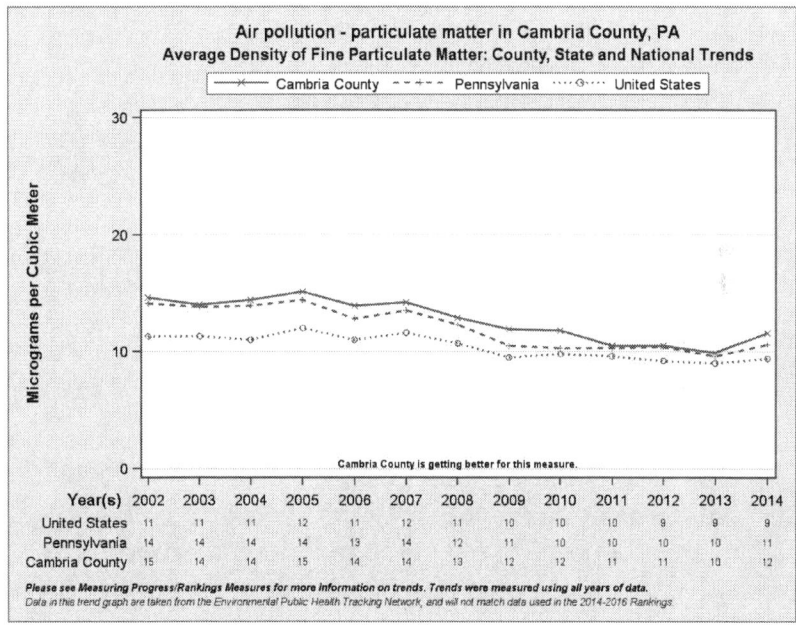

Figure 34, Trend in air quality for Cambria, PA, and U.S from 2002 to 2014 (Source County Health Rankings)

- With respect to the air quality, the county had 11.6 micrograms of particulate matter per cubic meter which was higher than the state rate of 10.6 and the U.S rate of 8.6. The county ranked 61st in the state on this measure. Figure 34 shows that after years of decline, there was an increase in particulate matter in 2014 in the county. The presence of fracking wells (see Figure 16) and of coal cogeneration plants to the west of the county could explain the poor air quality.
- Cambria was one of the 21 counties with drinking water violations in 2018.

- Eighty-two percent of county commuters were driving alone to work in the county from 2014-2018. This was higher than the state and U.S rate of 76%. In the county, the rate was 59% for African Americans, 63% for Hispanics, and 84% for Caucasians. The county ranked 21st in the state on this measure.
  - The average traffic volume per meter of major roadways in the county was 86 in 2018 which was well below the state rate of 255. The county ranked 32nd on this measure.
- The rate of those who have a long commute (more than 30 minutes) to work and drive alone (28%) was lower in the county from 2014-2018 than in the state (37%) and the U.S (36%). The county ranked 21st in the state on this measure.
- Twelve percent of people in the county have severe housing problems from 2012-2016 which was less than the state rate of 15% and the U.S rate of 18%. Of the 12%, ten percent of the total report a severe housing cost burden. The county ranked 35th in the state on this measure.
  - Seventy-four percent of the county residents owned their own home from 2014-2018 which was 5% higher than the state rate. The county was tied for 30th in the state on this measure.
  - Eleven percent of the county had a severe housing cost burden from 2014-2018 which was below the state rate of 13%. The county was tied for 29th on this measure in the state.

Racial disparities in health outcomes and increasing poverty are the biggest factors associated with the county's low health rankings in the state. As previously stated, about 59% of African Americans in the county live in Johnstown so disparities between the city and the rest of Cambria County also could also be a factor in the low ranking. It is impossible to address one disparity without addressing the others.

This list of statistics shows how many subtle nuances (not all of them bad) there are in these health rankings. One must always be careful in drawing cause and effect conclusions from correlational data. With Johnstown's declining population, it is now beginning to resemble a rural area with many abandoned houses. The disparities between the city and the county will be explored in the next chapter.

Corona Virus

Figure 35, Map of Pennsylvania showing Cambria County's first case of COVID-19 in medium red. Counties with more cases have a darker color (PA Department of Health) on April 27.

As I was updating this chapter with the new numbers from County Health Rankings, the world was amid the corona virus epidemic. On March 23, the county had its first confirmed case. This was 62 days after U.S. had its first case and 17 days after Pennsylvania its first case. Like everywhere else, the area has been practicing social distancing. On March 30 the county reported its second case, on April 1 the third and on April 2 the fourth.

As of this writing, the county had 21 cases, 959 total individuals who were tested, one patient on a ventilator, and one death. There are no cases in nursing homes to date. The case mortality rate (number of deaths divided by the number of cases) of 4.8% was higher for the county than the state rate of 3.8% but not the U.S. rate of 5.7%. The case mortality rate for the county was tied for the 16th highest in the state. The trend in cases is summarized in figure 36. So far, the most affected counties in the state are the most populated. It could be argued that the county's decrease in population has bought it time to prepare for the outbreak.

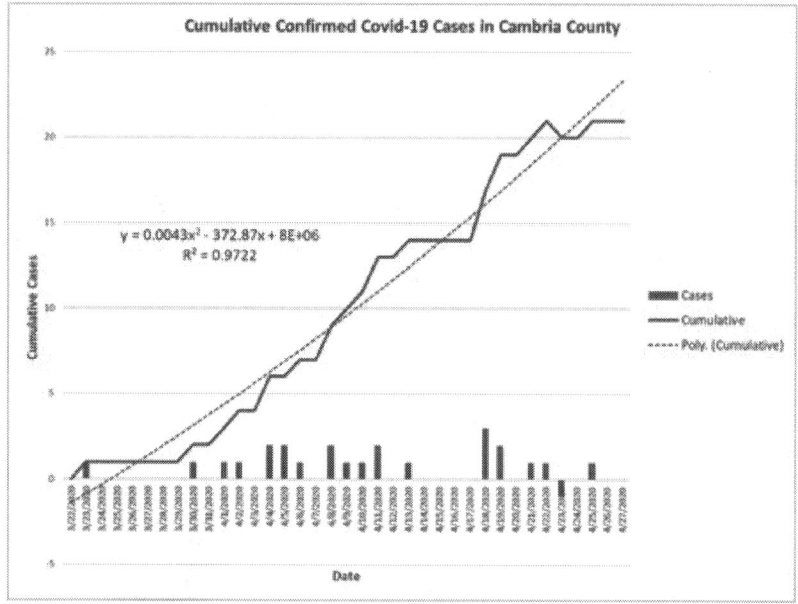

Figure 36a, Cumulative corona virus cases in Cambria County with third order polynomial trend line as reported by the PA Department of Health

Figure 36a is a graph I created for the number of cases reported by the Pennsylvania Department of Health. The bars represent the number of new cases reported that day. The solid line represents the increase in the cumulative cases. The dotted line represents the best fit quadratic trend line for the increase in cases. The equation for the trendline appears on the graph. The r-squared statistic shows the percentage in the variability in the number of new cases accounted for by the equation. This equation accounts for 96.19% of the variability in the cumulative case line. If 100% were accounted for, the dotted line would perfectly hug the cumulative case line.

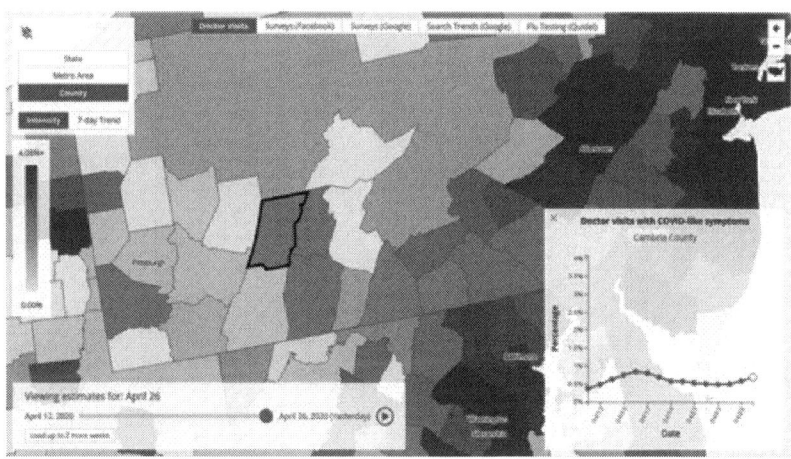

Figure 36b, Carnegie Mellon University's COVID-19 forecasting tool

There is no telling how long it will last but we are seeing the beginnings of an exponential growth curve. Carnegie Mellon University has an online analytics COVID-19 forecaster that the state will use to predict the trajectory of cases. It uses doctor visits, Google and Facebook surveys, and testing for the flu to predict the future trajectory of cases. Cambria County is highlighted in figure 36b with the graph showing the trend in doctor visits. Currently it predicts that the number of cases will be steady in the immediate future.

The most recent unemployment rate from February 2020 for the county is 5.7% which is higher than the state rate of 4.7% and the U.S. rate of 3.5%. Almost certainly, there will be a large increase in the area for the March 2020 state Unemployment report. The state unemployment report comes out a month after the U.S. rate for that month. For March 2020, the U.S. rate was 4.4%. Staying at home has given me more time to finish the book.

VIII. DISPARITIES BETWEEN JOHNSTOWN AND THE REST OF THE COUNTY

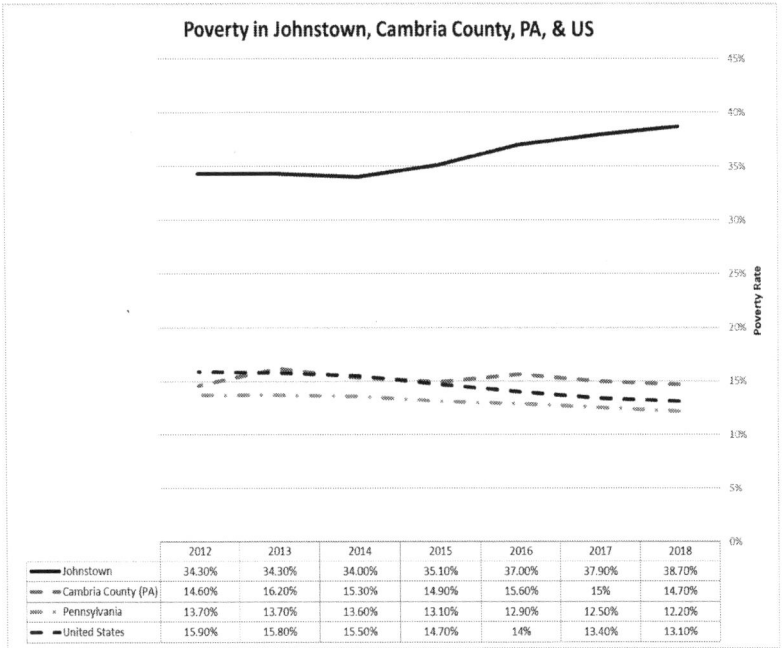

Figure 37a, Poverty Estimates from the Census Bureau for Johnstown, Cambria County, Pennsylvania and the U.S 2012-2018 (Source: Census Bureau)

The graph above shows estimated poverty rates from the Census Bureau's Small Area Income and Poverty Estimates (SAIPE) which is based on their annual American Community Survey. It shows that poverty rates in the city are more than double that of the county, state, and the U.S. and this gap has been growing since 2014. The trend in the city rate has increased since 2014. The county rate has been consistently higher than the state rate and since has been higher than the U.S rate since 2015.

PennLive magazine published a list of the 35 poorest towns in Pennsylvania using 2016 census data (Woodall, 2020). Johnstown ranked eighth in the state that year. Nearby Indiana Borough ranked first.

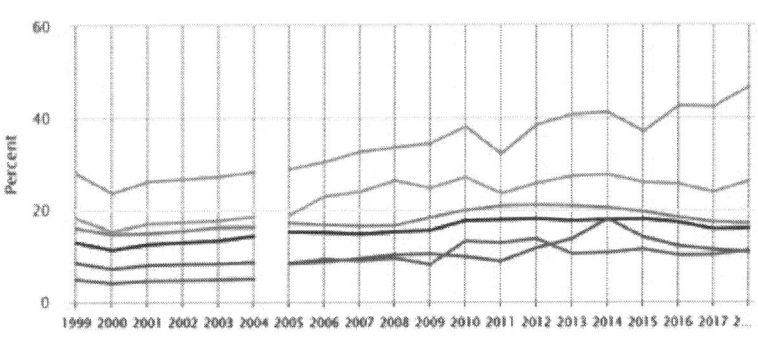

Figure 37b, Census Bureau poverty estimates for the Greater Johnstown, Ferndale, Richland, and Westmont School Districts and for the U.S and Pennsylvania, 1999-2018 (Source: Census Bureau)

The Census Bureau also provides estimates of the percentage of students in poverty in each of the 13,207 school districts in the U.S. for their students from the ages of 5-17. In 2018 the Greater Johnstown School District (GJSD) had an estimated 46.7% of their student body below the poverty level. In figure 36b we can see that this trend has been increasing steadily since 1999. This is the highest estimate in the state and well ahead of the neighboring districts of Ferndale (26.2%), Richland (10.7%), and Westmont (11.0%) and of the U.S (17.0%) and the PA rate (15.9%). Nationally GJSD ranks 84th or in the 99th percentile of all of the school districts in the U.S.

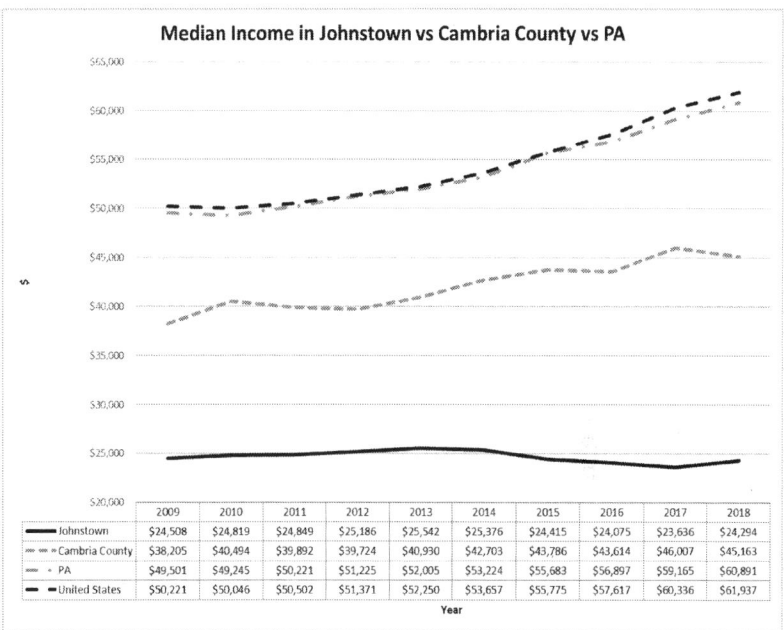

Figure 37c, Median household income for Johnstown, Cambria County, Pennsylvania and the U.S. for 2009-2017

The Census Bureau also provides median household income estimates for the city, county, state, and the U.S. Johnstown's median income stagnated after the Great Recession and, just as the poverty rate increased after 2014, it decreased after 2014. The county median income, while lagging the state and U.S rate, did increase along with the state and U.S median incomes in 2017, followed by a decrease in 2018. The state and the U.S incomes were nearly identical over this period. The city was named as the poorest in the state based on the 2016 numbers in Figure 36c (Stebbins and Sauter, 2019). The article by Stebbins and Sauter goes on to state that 38.8% of people in the city qualified for SNAP benefits or food stamps.

Sauter (2019) also looked at the poverty numbers for Johnstown for 2018 and found that Johnstown was the seventh poorest city in the U.S. Centerville, Illinois was first. In addition to the 2018 numbers presented here, Sauter (2019) presents statistics showing that 12% of the city has a bachelor's degree and the median home value was $41,000.

Trends in Crime in the City, the County, the State and the U.S

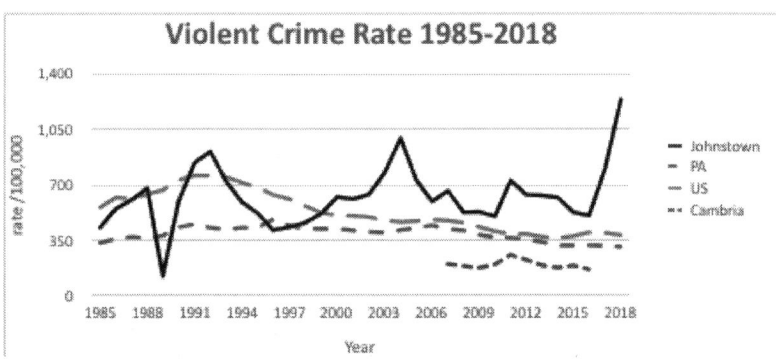

Figure 38a, Violent Crime Rates in Johnstown, Cambria County, Pennsylvania, and the U.S. from 1985-2018

The FBI Uniform Crime Report (UCR) (2019a) is an annual census of crime conducted by the FBI where almost every police department in the U.S. participates. Figure 37a shows the rate of reported violent crimes in the City of Johnstown, Cambria County, Pennsylvania, and the U.S. Violent crimes include homicide, rape, robbery, and aggravated assault. The graph shows that the population adjusted rate in the city has been higher than the state and U.S rates since 1999 with a sharp increase since 2016. Figure 37a shows that the rate for the county is lower than the state and U.S rates from 2007-2016.

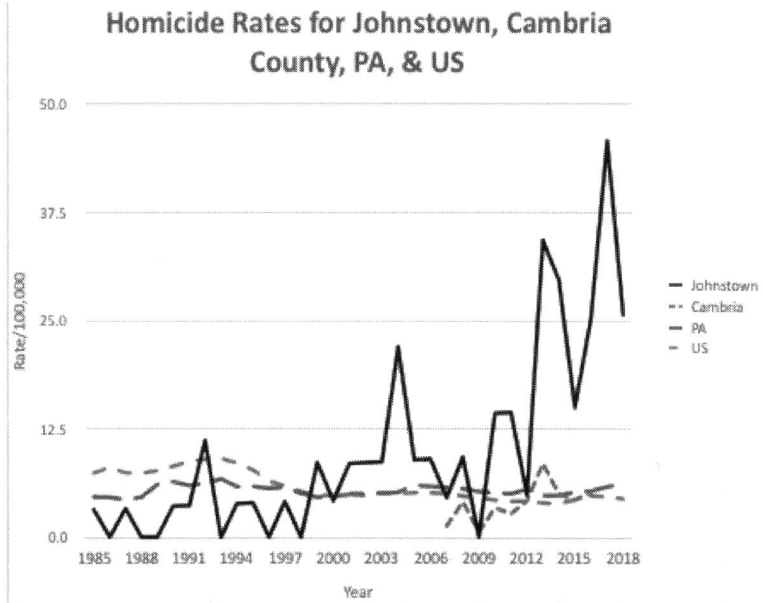

Figure 38b, Homicide Rates in Johnstown Proper, Cambria County, Pennsylvania, and the U.S from 1985-2018

Figure 37b shows that the homicide rate for the city has risen above the state and U.S rates in 2015 with a peak in 2017. There were nine total homicides inside the city limits that year. The county rate is only available from 2007-2016 (State Police website, 2019) but it does more closely reflect the state and U.S rates for this period.

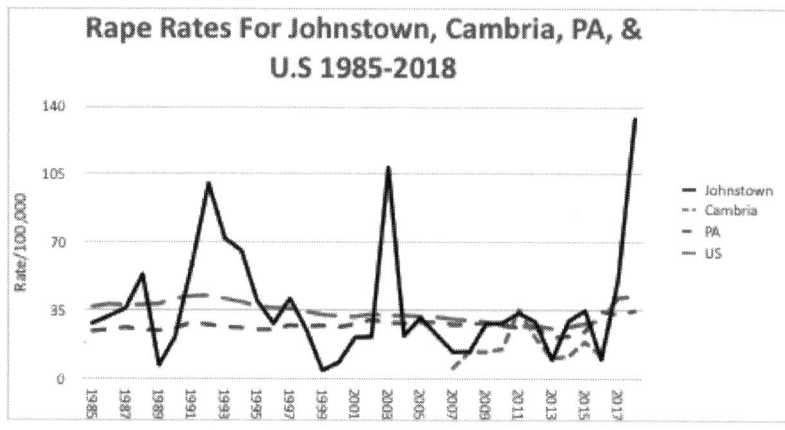

Figure 38c, Rates of Reported Rapes for Johnstown, Cambria, PA, and U.S 1985-2018

Figure 37c looks at reported rapes in the Johnstown, Cambria, the state and the U.S. The city rates were close to the county, state, and U.S. except for peaks in 1988, 1992-1995, 2003 and 2017-2018. As with the other categories, data at the county level are only available for 2007-2016. The state and U.S. rates for 2017 and 2018 are adjusted rape rates. Prior to that they are called legacy rates by the FBI. Legacy rape rates (or the old rape definition) are defined by the FBI defined as "the carnal knowledge of a female forcibly and against her will." The adjusted rape rates are for the new definition which states; "penetration, no matter how slight, of the vagina or anus with any body part or object, or oral penetration by a sex organ of another person, without the consent of the victim. Attempts or assaults to commit rape are also included; however, statutory rape and incest are excluded" (FBI, 2019b). Rape is always a notoriously underreported crime but this broader definition could account for the increase at the state and national level. The rise in Johnstown's rate does outpace the increase in the U.S. and PA rates.

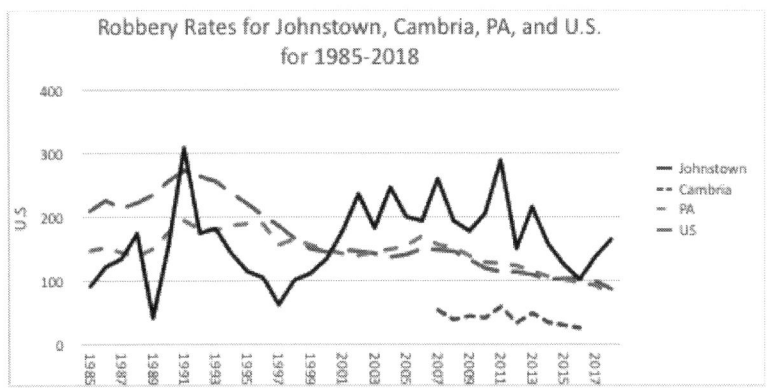

Figure 38d, Rates of Robbery for Johnstown, Cambria, PA, and U.S 1985-2018

Robbery is the fourth component of the FBIs violent crime statistics. Figure 37d shows elevated rates for Johnstown from 2001 to 2014 with another spike in 2018. Cambria county overall had a lower rate than the state and the U.S at least from 2007-2016. Looking at all four types of crimes it seems that the rates of aggravated assault, rape, and homicide are what are driving the recent spike in overall violent crime rates.

Differences Between the Johnstown, Westmont, and Richland School Districts in Special Education Burdens

The Pennsylvania State Data Center issues an annual report (2019) on Special Education data for each school district in the state. For this book I will take a look at the Greater Johnstown, Westmont, and Richland School Districts for the '07-'08 and '18-'19 school years. My purpose is to show changes in enrollment and the special education population over the last 11 years. The state rates are provided for comparison.

Table 6
Trends in School Enrollment and Special Education Needs for the Greater Johnstown, Richland, and Westmont School Districts (NR=Not Reported)

	Greater Johnstown		Richland		Westmont		State	
	'07-'08	'18-'19	'07-'08	'18-'19	'07-'08	'18-'19	'07-'08	'18-'19
% special Ed	19%	17.90%	10.10%	11.00%	9.40%	14.10%	15.2%	17.30%
Total Enrollment	3,027	2,886	1,633	1,506	1,720	1,470	1,801,760	1,723,405
% Caucasian (total)	67.00%	45%	96.10%	90.70%	96.60%	87.10%	73.9%	64.6%
% Caucasian (Sp. ed.)	70.80%	49%	95.20%	89.20%	96.30%	79.70%	NR	63.1%
% African American (total)	29.80%	34%	1.00%	2.50%	1.20%	2.10%	16.0%	14.8%
% African American (Sp. ed.)	27.10%	33%	NR	6.60%	NR	NR	NR	17.8%
Specific Disabilities (% of all special ed)								
Intellectual Disability	7.10%	6.80%	12.70%	9.00%	7.50%	8.70%	8.50%	6.30%
Autism	NR	10.30%	NR	15.70%	NR	18.40%	4.60%	11.30%
Learning Disability	49.20%	34.70%	49.70%	39.80%	53.40%	38.60%	52.10%	40.60%
Emotional Disturbance	11.50%	13.80%	0.00%	8.50%	7.50%	11.10%	9.40%	8.50%
Speech or Language Impairment	18.40%	13.00%	14.50%	7.80%	15.50%	10.10%	16.10%	14.30%

Table 6 above shows that enrollment in each school district and in the state overall has decreased. Statewide it has decreased by 4.3%, while in Greater Johnstown it has decreased 4.7%, in Richland it has decreased 7.8%, and in Westmont it has decreased 14.5% over this time period. The percentage of enrollment in special education increased from 15% to 17.3% statewide. In Greater Johnstown, it decreased from 19% to 17.9% over the same period, while in Richland it increased from 10.1% to 11%, and in Westmont it increased from 9.4% to 14.1%. The Greater Johnstown School District has a larger special ed percentage than the state and the more affluent neighboring Richland and Westmont School Districts.

The starkest change in the enrollment for Greater

Johnstown School District is in its ethnic makeup. In the '07-'08 school year the district was 67% Caucasian. Ten years later it was 45%, a 22% decrease. The African American percentage increased from 29.8% to 34% over this period while Hispanic enrollment increased from 1.8% to 4.2% at the same time. The remainder of the student body or 16% is identified as multiracial in 2018. This category was not reported in '07-'08.

For special education, African Americans were 27.1% of the total in '07-'08 and 33% in '18-'19 which is 1% lower than their representation in the student body. Caucasians were 70.8% of special education students in '07-'08 which was 3.8% higher than it was in the student body and in '18-'19 they were 49% of the total which is 4% higher than their representation in the student body. 13.8% of special ed students were multiracial in '18-'19 which is 2.2% lower than their percentage in the student body.

In Richland the % Caucasian decreased from 96.1% in '07-'08 to 90.7% in '18-'19. The % African American increased from 1% to 2.5% and the % Hispanic increased from 1% to 1.9% over this period. Two-point three percent of those enrolled identified as multiracial in '18-'19. Ninety-five percent of those in special education were Caucasian in '07-'08 while 89.2% were in '18-'19. African Americans were less than 1% of special education students there in '07-'08 while in '18-'19 there were 6.6% of the total which is 4.1% higher than their percentage in the student body.

In Westmont the percentage of Caucasians in the student body decreased from 96.6% in '07-'08 to 87.1% in '18-'19. The percentage of African Americans increased from 1.2% to 2.1% and the percentage of Hispanics increased from 0.7% to 2.9% over this period. The percentage of those identified as multiracial were 6.5% in '18-'19. The special education students were 96.3% Caucasian in '07-'08 and 79.7% in '18-'19, for an underrepresentation of 0.3% and 7.4% respectively. For African Americans, the percentage in special education was not reported in '07-'08 or in '18-'19. For Hispanics, the percentage in special education was not reported in '07-'08, but in '18-'19 it was 5.3%. This is 2.4% higher than the student body. Multiracial special education students were 8.7% of the total which is 2.2% higher than the student body in the year '18-'19.

If we look at changes in the types of disabilities served, statewide there was a decrease in the percentage of students with intellectual (-2.2%) and learning (-11.5%) disabilities, speech and/or language impairments (-1.8) and emotional disturbances (-0.9%). There was a 6.7% increase in the percentage of special ed students with autism.

- In Greater Johnstown there were decreases in intellectual (-0.3) and learning (-14.5%) disabilities and in speech and/or language impairments (-5.4%). There were increases in autism (10.3%) and emotional disturbance (2.3%).
- At Richland there were likewise decreases in the percentage of intellectual (-3.7%) and learning (-15%) disabilities and in speech and/or language impairments (-7.7%). There were increases in autism (15.7%) and emotional disturbance (8.5%).
- At Westmont there was a decrease in the percentage of learning disabilities (-14.8%) and speech and/or language impairments (-4.4%) and an increase in the percentage of students with intellectual disabilities (1.2%), autism (18.4%), and emotional disturbance (3.6%).

This could mostly reflect the fact that autism is diagnosed now a lot more often than it has been in the past.

Political Differences Between the City and County in 2016 and Beyond

When I returned to Johnstown in March 2016, I came to organize for Bernie Sanders (and for personal reasons) for the Pennsylvania Primary on April 27. At the first campaign meeting on April 7 we had 30 people (Figure 38). We were busy canvassing, phone banking and leafleting the county. We were happy to receive a lot of positive feedback from the people to whom we spoke. Pennsylvania has a closed primary system where only voters registered in their political parties can vote in their respective primaries which put us at a disadvantage as Sanders was more successful in states with open primaries.

Figure 39, The first Johnstown meeting of the campaign for Bernie Sanders

When the primary came Hillary Clinton had won the state with large majorities in Pittsburgh and Philadelphia. Overall, she had won the state by the same margin that she had in the 2008 primary against Barack Obama, 55% to 45%. In 2008, Obama only won seven counties (including Philadelphia County) in the state and managed to garner 45% of the vote. In 2016, Sanders won 31 out of 67 counties (mostly in the center of the state) to earn 45% of the vote.

Clinton won Cambria County in 2008 with 72% of the vote. In 2016, Bernie Sanders won the county by 537 votes with 46.9% of the vote (Table 7) in spite of former President Clinton making a stop to the Pitt Johnstown Campus. On the Republican side Trump won the county and the state with 65% of the vote in the county. Turnout was higher for the Republicans than for the Democrats. In Johnstown Hillary Clinton won the city 1,227 votes to 977 for Sanders, a margin of 250 votes. Sanders won 5 of the 20 precincts in the city.

Table 7
2016 Democratic Presidential Primary Results in Cambria County

Candidate	Percent	Votes
Hillary **CLINTON**	**44%**	8304
Bernie **SANDERS**	**46.9%**	8841
Roque Rocky De La **FUENTE**	**2.6%**	499
WRITE-IN	**6.4%**	1213

Figure 40, The PA 35th State Senatorial District (PA Department of State)

Changes in Voter Registration in Cambria County 2014-2018

In my blog, *CSI without Dead Bodies,* I looked at how voter registration patterns have changed in the county since 2014 to March 2020. For comparison I also looked at changes in the county population over the same period. Gains for Republicans in the county were strongest between 2014 and 2016 but slowed in the period leading up to the 2018 midterms and then increased as of March 2020. For the Democrats, these losses have accelerated after the 2016 election far outstripping losses in county population. Third parties and independents gained in the period between 2014 and 2016 but lost registrants in the lead up to 2018 and 2020.

Table 8
Changes in Cambria County Voter Registration 2014-2020

Cambria County	2014	2016	2018	2020	% Change '14-'16	% Change '14-'18	% Change '14-'20
Democrat	48,417	45,378	41,332	38,439	-6.4	-14.7	-20.6
Republican	27,475	32,756	33,261	35,613	19.2	21.1	29.6
Other	8,287	8,714	8,580	8,551	5.2	3.5	3.2
Population	137,386	134,313	131,370	130,192	-2.2	-4.4	-5.2

The 2016 General Election in Johnstown

After the primary, I worked for Ed Cernic's State Senate campaign as a field organizer for District 35. He became the Democratic nominee after the incumbent, John Wozniak, withdrew after winning the primary for his seat. A survey showed Wozniak had no chance of winning. Gerrymandering is a factor in State House and Senate races as well as U.S. House races. The district included all of Cambria County, Bedford County and most of Clearfield County (Figure 39).

Cernic was the Cambria County Controller. His opponent was Wayne Langerholc, an assistant District Attorney for Cambria County. Cernic's strategy was to run as a conservative pro-gun, pro-death penalty, and anti-abortion Democrat. The County's two Democratic state Representatives, Bryan Barbin and Frank Burns, ran on a similar platform. They worked tirelessly to distance themselves from Hillary Clinton. In the Pennsylvania State House and in the State Senate, Republicans would gain a super majority in this election.

Donald Trump came to the city on October 21, 2016. He filled the Cambria County War Memorial Arena to almost capacity with 6,001 supporters. Trump promised "Your Jobs will come back (Sutor, 2016)" in the coal and steel industries. He received thunderous applause. All of the Republican candidates in the county, including Langerholc, spoke at his rally. Hillary Clinton did visit the city in an invitation only event in the summer (Musselman, 2016).

When Election Day came Cernic lost to Langerholc 63% to 37%. The result was closest in Cambria County with Langerholc winning 54% to 46%. Langerholc had 79% of the vote in Bedford County and 67% in Clearfield. Barbin and Burns won their races for State Rep in the county.

The election result that received the most attention by far was Donald Trump's victory in the central part of the state. His showing was enough to overcome the strong majority that Clinton had in Pittsburgh and Philadelphia, winning the state by 45,000 votes. In Cambria County, he won by 67% to 30% for Clinton or, in terms of the vote total, 42,258 to 18,867. This was the largest margin of victory in the county for a presidential candidate since the 1964 landslide win of Lyndon Johnson (Whittle, 2007).

The news media was astounded that a county that had once been so reliably democratic could vote so overwhelmingly for Trump. It had voted for the Democratic candidate for President in every election from 1960 to 2000. It was close in 2004, 2008 and 2012 for George W. Bush, Barack Obama, and Mitt Romney respectively. Once again looking inside the election numbers shows that there was a disconnect between the city of Johnstown and the rest of Cambria County.

The result inside the city limits of Johnstown was different than the rest of the county. Hillary Clinton won the city by 83 votes or 1.3% of the vote. As seen in Appendix C, she won 11 of the precincts with her strongest showing in the predominantly African American precinct of Prospect, followed by the 7th ward, and the second precinct in Johnstown's center city. Trump's strongest showings were in the third precinct of the 8th ward and in the 21st ward.

IX. DOCUMENTARY FILMMAKERS DESCEND UPON JOHNSTOWN

In the aftermath of the 2016 election the news media descended upon Johnstown asking the question: How could such a reliably Democratic county like Cambria vote so overwhelmingly for Donald Trump? This included the BBC (2016), ABC (2016), and Politico magazine (2017). They relied on person on the street interviews and on interviews with community leaders.

Katie Couric

The most famous of these journalists who came to Johnstown was Katie Couric (2018), formerly of the Today Show and the CBS Evening News. She was working on a documentary for the National Geographic Channel called America Inside Out. The episode in her series focused was titled White Anxiety. The city leaders rolled out the red carpet for her to show the city in the best possible light. She focused on the opioid epidemic here and the struggles that families have. She quoted statistics showing that divorce rates were higher for those without a college education and were rising nationally. She did not present local statistics.

Gary Younge

The next documentary filmmaker who came here was Gary Younge. He is a writer for The Nation magazine and The Guardian newspaper in London, England. Their project was interviewing people from Portland, Maine to Louisiana about their economic situation for the documentary Angry, White, and American. I met with one of his researchers to give him a layout of the land. He told me they were looking for people to interview who recently lost jobs in the steel mills. I told him that the mills left in the 1980s. I showed him the local soup kitchens and homeless shelters. I haven't seen this documentary, so I don't know what was said.

Siobahn Furnary and Hunter Zepeda

Figure 41, Screenshot from With the Rain

A third filmmaker group who came to the city were Siobahn Furnary and Hunter Zepeda from Oberlin College working on a project titled With the Rain (2018). Their focus was on how the faith community in Johnstown addressed the social needs of the community. The documentary consisted of still shots of various parts of the city. Some were of beautiful churches. Others were of run-down churches, closed schools, and other scenes from around town. Those being interviewed were not shown on screen, but one could hear their voices. Katherine-Anne McCloskey, the grand-niece of Johnstown mayor Eddie McCloskey, was one of those interviewed. The opinions expressed in the film ranged from optimistic to pessimistic.

Vince Grassi

The fourth recent documentary on Johnstown is titled This Town Won't Die by Vince Grassi (2020). The website for the film states that:

This Town Won't Die is an investigative/sports docudrama that dives into the inner city of Johnstown, Pennsylvania. The documentary questions the status quo and available opportunities in this once roaring American community.

Johnstown, Pennsylvania has become an image of modern-day adversity. The youth community and the struggles some (Greater Johnstown Area School District Students) are susceptible to, has become evident in recent times. There are many issues in question. These issues include: the economic state, after school programs for the youth, bullying, violence, drug and poverty factors. The movie's main underpinning questions current day political motives and who becomes the chess pieces in American community scenarios.

I was interviewed by Vince Grassi for the film. The film was released in 2020. It can be viewed on Vimeo.

Changes in the AAABA Tournament

On a lighter note, the All American Amateur Baseball Association or AAABA has had its annual tournament here in Johnstown since 1945, with the exception of 1946 when it was held in Washington, DC, and in 1977 when it was held in Altoona due to the flood of 1977. Amateur teams from around the eastern half of the U.S come to the city to compete for the championship. Players from the tournament such as Rod Carew, John Smoltz, Steve Garvey and Joe Torre went on to Hall of Fame careers in the major leagues. Baltimore won the tournament the most times with 29 wins followed by New Orleans with 16 wins and Washington with 10. Baltimore and Washington no longer send teams to the tournament.

The tournament had a double elimination format where if a team lost two games they were eliminated. In 2009 the tournament allowed a city to send more than one team to the tournament thus improving Johnstown's chance of winning. Johnstown now sent two teams to the tournament. Also, in 2016 the tournament switched to a group play format where teams who won their individual group after three games would play in a single elimination playoff format.

Figure 42, The crowd at the Point Stadium for the 1971 AAABA Tournament

The Johnstown team in the tournament always has its games at the Point Stadium at night where the tournament makes most if its money (Figure 41). Crowds came to the stadium as long as the Johnstown team was not eliminated in the tournament. Changing the format of the tournament allowed both Johnstown teams to play at least three games at the Point, especially after the size of the stadium shrunk to hold 7,500 spectators.

The first Johnstown entrant that participated in every tournament had a record of 148 wins and 145 losses or a 50.5% winning percentage for the whole history of the tournament. The second Johnstown team has a record of 22 wins and 25 losses for a percentage of 48.8% and finished second twice. The first Johnstown entrant finished second six times, two of them after 2009. In 2018, the 74th anniversary of the tournament, Martella's Pharmacy (the first Johnstown entrant that year) of Johnstown finally won the Tournament with a record of 6 wins and no losses beating New Orleans 3-2. In the 75th edition Martella's made it to the championship game again but lost to New Orleans 5-2 for a total of nine second place finishes for the city. This would make a great subject for a documentary.

Figure 43, Martella's won the first AAABA for Johnstown

X. RUNNING FOR CITY COUNCIL AND THE 2018 MIDTERM ELECTION

Figure 44, A city council meeting to discuss Bill 5

In 2017, I took it upon myself to run for the Johnstown City Council. The council was considering Bill 5, an ordinance to ban discrimination against LGBTQ individuals in the city. The state has no such law. A large crowd came to the first meeting in March 2017 where the bill was being considered (Figure 43) both pro and con for the bill. The measure was tabled at that meeting and in two subsequent monthly meetings.

Four of the six council members plus the mayor were up for reelection that year. At the first meeting after the Democratic primary in June, Bill 5 was voted down 6 to 1. The mayor, Frank Janakovic, and council members Nunzio Johncola, David Vitovich, Jack Williams, Pete Vizza, and Charlene Stanton voted "no." Only Marie Mock voted "yes" (Pesto, 2017).

The primary featured one Republican and about nine Democrats for city council. There were three candidates for mayor, incumbent Frank Janakovic, City Councilman Jack Williams, and local activist John DeBartola. Janakovic won the primary for mayor and for city council the winners were: Sylvia King, Marie Mock, David Vitovich, and Ricky Britt.

In response to the primary and to the disappointment over Bill 5, I decided to run as an independent for city council. I ran on this platform:

- A living wage ordinance for the city.

- I was going to propose a living wage ordinance, but it was brought to my attention that Pennsylvania has a law preventing cities from doing so. As a city councilman, I would have introduced a resolution urging the state and federal government to do so.
* End corruption by improving enforcement and transparency in city government.
* Body cameras for police.
* City wide Wi-Fi.
* Consolidation of local communities with Johnstown.
* Fight the drug problem in the city through better treatment and education

I kept my campaign spending under $250. I relied on leafleting and social media to get my message out. The race was for four at large council seats and one mayoral position. In the last few weeks of the campaign Councilwoman Charlene Stanton announced a write-in campaign for mayor. I challenged the other candidates to have a debate or a candidate forum and received no response. There were such events during the primary campaign. All of the candidates were interviewed by the Johnstown Tribune-Democrat. The paper endorsed the four Democrats in the race. The results of the election can be seen in Table 9.

Table 9
City Council General Election Results for Johnstown. Voters could vote for up to four candidates

Candidate	Percent of votes cast (n=8,633)	Votes	% of voters (n=2,179)
Sylvia J. King (Democrat)	20.80%	1,792	82.24%
Ricky Britt (Democrat)	18.90%	1,629	74.76%
Marie A. Mock (Democrat)	19.70%	1,702	78.11%
David Vitovich (Democrat)	19.10%	1,647	75.59%
Mark Amsdell (Republican)	11.60%	1,003	46.03%
Paul Ricci (Independent)	8.90%	765	35.11%
Write-in (No Party Specified)	1.10%	95	4%

I had received 765 votes. Voters could vote for up to four candidates. Many voters voted straight Democrat or straight Republican. There were 8,633 total votes cast. Because voters could vote for up to four candidates in this race, there were 2,179 total voters in the race. When dividing by the total voters I received 35.11% of the total voters. Looking at the 20 precincts in the city, my best showing percentagewise was 11.6% in the 2nd and 3rd precincts in the 8th ward (the Roxbury sections of town). This makes sense as I had volunteers working the polls all day there on that cold rainy/snowy day as the picture below shows (Figure 44). Charlene Stanton received 495 write in votes for Mayor.

Figure 45, A Poll worker and the author (on the left) on Election Day 2017

The 2018 Election

Nationally, the 2018 midterm elections were seen by Democrats as a landslide for women in the House of Representatives. Trump would point to Republican gains in the U.S Senate to refute this claim. The picture here in Johnstown and Cambria County would be very different from the state and the U.S.

Statewide the Democrats had an advantage in voter registration but the Republicans controlled 13 of the state's 18 congressional districts prior to the 2018 election (see Figure 45a). In the midst of the primary campaign in 2018, the State Supreme Court redrew the boundaries of the 18 congressional districts in the state to make the districts less biased towards Republicans.

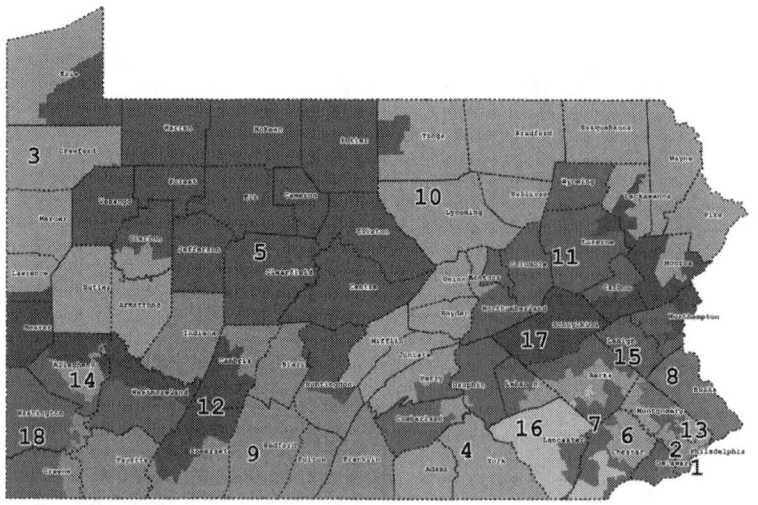

Figure 45a-PA Congressional Districts from 2012 to 2017 (Wikipedia)

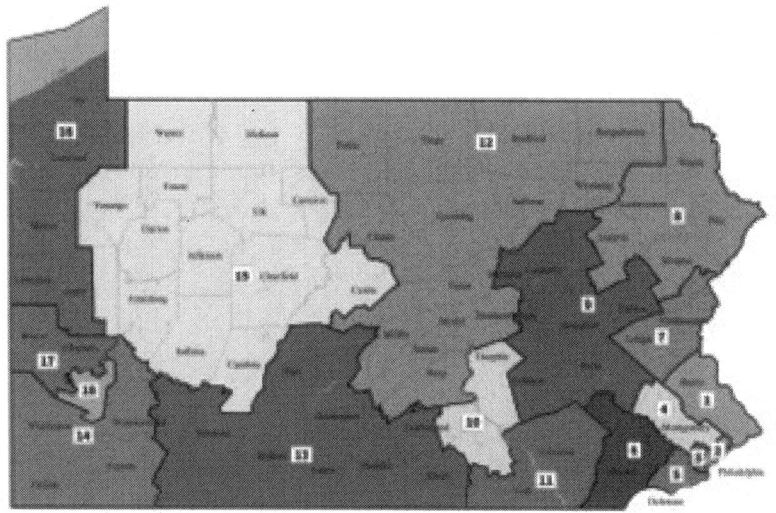

Figure 46b-PA Congressional Districts 2018-2020 (PA Department of State)

Prior to the redistricting, Republican Keith Rothfus represented most of Cambria County in the 12th District with Republican Bill Shuster representing its upper northeast corner in the ninth district (Figure 45a). Figure 45b shows that, after the redistricting, the lower southwest corner of the county, which includes Johnstown, was now in Bill Shuster's district which stretched from Westmoreland County to Adams County where Gettysburg is located. The rest of the county was now in Glenn Thompson's district which stretches from Cambria County to the New York state line.

Bill Shuster decided not to run for reelection. The candidates for the district were the anti-abortion Republican physician John Joyce and the middle of the road Democrat Brent Ottaway. Glenn Thompson was being challenged by IUP (Indiana University of PA) Professor Susan Boser. Joyce won his race 70%-30% while Thompson won 68% to 32%. Statewide, Democrats picked up four seats in U.S House races to make the ratio of Republicans to Democrats nine to nine. Previously it had been 13 to 5 in favor of Republicans.

U.S Senator Bob Casey and Governor Tom Wolf were also up for reelection that year. They won their races with 55% and 57% of the vote respectively. Casey was running against Congressman Lou Barletta of Hazleton and Wolf was running against State Senator Scott Wagner. However, Casey and Wolf both lost Cambria County by large margins.

The State House races in the county showed a further shift to the Republicans while Democrats gained statewide. Democrat Bryan Barbin lost to Republican Jim Rigby (brother of WJAC-TV anchor Tim Rigby) 52%-48%. Democrat Frank Burns survived a challenge from Republican Jerry Carnicella by the same percentage margin by which Barbin lost.

XI. ACTIVISTS WORKING TO TURN THE CITY AROUND

It is depressing to see the economic and health statistics of Johnstown. There are many groups of people in the area trying to turn the fortunes of the city around. These groups include health care activists, the unity coalition to improve racial relations in the community, the Population Health Center by Thomas Jefferson University, individuals working to win the right to receive compensation from the Catholic Church over abuse by clergy, those looking to expose corruption in the city, and those looking to improve the art scene here in the county. These groups are in addition to the national organizations that are present in the area.

Non-Profits in Johnstown

I made a search of the website Guidestar, which lists all non-profit organizations in the U.S. This search of the organizations that list Johnstown as their home base turned up 494 organizations. These organizations have Johnstown listed as their mailing address and do not necessarily reside within the city limits.

Sorting these organizations by their gross receipts, as reported by the IRS master file, reveals the Concurrent Technologies Corporation (CTC) as having the most receipts earning $85,696,067 and having $61,158,212 in assets. The top non-profit organizations in gross receipts are listed in Table 10. Of the organizations in the top 10, The Community Foundation for the Alleghenies and Goodwill of the Southern Alleghenies have silver ratings from Guidestar while The Learning Lamp, Inc. has a platinum rating. These ratings reflect the organizations commitment to transparency. Of the 494 nonprofits listed, 48.6% or 240 report no receipts or assets to the IRS.

Table 10
Top 10 Earning Non-Profit Organizations in Johnstown

Name	Gross Receipts	Assets
Concurrent Technologies Corporation	$85,696,067	$61,158,212
Behavioral Health of Cambria County	$41,622,034	$11,020,878
Cambria County Assoc. for the Blind & Handicapped	$19,132,845	$61,399,004
Goodwill of the Southern Alleghenies	$16,625,200	$16,491,687
Arbutus Park Manor	$14,522,631	$17,309,938
Citizens Cemetery Association	$13,228,953	$11,996,146
Alternative Community Resource Program	$12,099,811	$6,523,614
Community Foundation for the Alleghenies	$11,106,789	$68,269,600
Community Action Partnership of Cambria County	$10,351,613	$2,446,242
The Learning Lamp	$8,753,639	$1,780,992

Foundations in the Area

Community Foundation for the Alleghenies

The Community Foundation for the Alleghenies provides grants and scholarships to deserving non-profits and individuals in Bedford, Cambria, and Somerset Counties. Started in 1990 the foundation has funded initiatives called the 2018-22 Strategic Plan, Lift Johnstown, the Penelec Sustainable Energy Fund, the Speakers Bureau, Vision2025, and the Youth Philanthropy Internship Program. Mark Pasquerilla serves as board chair and Mike Kane serves as Foundation President and Executive Director. Kane is also active with the FrakTracker Alliance that was discussed in Chapter 6.

1889 Foundation

Founded in 1993 the 1889 Foundation is dedicated to improving the health of people in the region. The foundation was originally part of the Conemaugh

Memorial Medical Center but when the medical center was bought up by Duke LifePoint it became an independent 501c3 organization in 2015. It funds the 1889 Jefferson Center for Population Health described below. It also funds blight alleviation in Johnstown's West End, Communities in Schools at the Greater Johnstown School District, the Cambria City Cultural Partnership, and the Cambria County Drug Coalition. Unlike the Community Foundation for the Alleghenies, the 1889 Foundation does not list its assets on its website. According to Guidestar it has $11,692,806 in assets.

Glosser Foundation

The David A. Glosser Foundation, named after the family, that founded Glosser Brothers department store, has no website. According to Guidestar it has $1,787,945 in assets and it began in 1963.

Vision 2025

Vision 2025 came about as a result of Carnegie Mellon University's Remaking Cities Institute study of the city in 2015. The Vision 20205 website states that it is "A framework for revitalizing Greater Johnstown based upon an open, collaborative, and community-driven approach (Remaking Cities Institute, 2015)." It is a volunteer organization with three arms: a strong sense of community group, a life sustaining landscapes group, and a vibrant and open local economy group. These three groups are connected to a Vision 2025 governance committee. Capture teams are offshoots of these groups. They work to achieve one facet of the group's objectives. Examples of capture teams include Community Gardens, Bikes and Trails, Greenspace, Rivers, Central Park, Re-Energize Johnstown, and United Neighborhood. Each group has a specific focus which will be summarized here.

The study on which Vision 2025 (2015) is based listed as assets for the city:
- The region's character, people.
- Major institutions.
- The juxtaposition of the natural and industrial.
- A series of urban villages.
- The small scale of the city.
- Tourism.

Liabilities for the city were listed as:
- Flooding.
- A loss of industry.
- A lack of riverfront access.
- A culture of dependence expecting a "white knight" to save the city.
- Crime and drugs.
- A lack of unity.
- Urban blight.
- Inadequate career readiness.
- Unemployment.

The strategies they advocate for turning around the area are:
- Developing eco-tourism.
- Restore and protect water quality.
- Work for better passenger rail.
- Create more integrated educational opportunities.
- Develop a Conemaugh Valley watershed plan.
- Promote cultural assets and values.

Strategies to develop the city are:
- Introduce a mix of uses meaning having a wide variety of businesses.
- Develop linking anchors such as central park.
- Making a good first impression.

Galen Newman, a Texas A&M researcher in urban planning and landscape architecture, is now working with Vision 2025 to suggest new strategies to revitalize the city (Siwy, 2017). He uses spatial analytics of three-dimensional maps of the area to suggest new strategies to improve the built environment of the city. He has had successful efforts to improve Houston, TX and Dayton, OH. It remains to be seen what he will do for the area.

814 Worx

814 Worx is a cooperative where entrepreneurs can rent office space and conference rooms for less than the cost of renting an individual office. Its name comes from the 814 area code where Johnstown is located. It is a business incubator where high speed internet, office space, and a conference room are provided. It is located in the Feeder Canal building on Main Street downtown and is run by Ethan Stewart.

Unity Coalition of the Southern Alleghenies

The Unity Coalition of the Southern Alleghenies was founded in 1994 as a part of a statewide effort to counteract hate groups. It once had 43 chapters across the state. Two hundred one members signed a pledge to "promote respect for difference, to repudiate words and acts of hatred intimidation and violence, and to take a public stand for equality, diversity and nonviolence. (Unity Coalition Charter, 1994)" They had committees for: programming and community education, emergency response/supportive services, media/public relations, and heritage projects. They had bimonthly and later monthly meetings. Interest forms were given to members to see which committees on which they wanted to serve. The frequencies of their responses are shown in table 11.

Table 11
Frequencies of Interest to Serve on Different Committees in the Unity Coalition of the Southern Alleghenies

Interest Level	Programming and Community Education	Emergency Response/Supportive Services	Media/ Public Relations	Heritage Projects
Most Interested	5	3	2	4
Somewhat Interested	5	3	4	4
Least Interested	1	4	2	1
Not Interested	0	0	1	0

The above table shows that the committee that drew the most interest from those who filled out the survey was in the Programming and Community Education committee. This was followed by the Heritage Projects committee. The Emergency Response/Supportive Services and Media/Public Relations committees drew the least interest.

The coalition was galvanized in response to the efforts of Anabaptist Bishop Ron McCrae's and the KKK (then run by Barry Black and C. Everett Foster) to drive out a gay bar called the Casa Nova just across the county line in Somerset County in 1997 (Pittsburgh Lesbian Correspondents, 2006; Levine, 2006). Prior to these events they had roughly a dozen people attend their meeting. Afterwards that number roughly doubled. By November 2000 they had 151 members on file. They hosted many film series and cultural events and community gardens in the Kernville section of town (Johnstown Area Heritage Association (JAHA) archives, 2017). The FBI reported a decrease in hate group activity in the area by 2002 (Marcus, 2002).

The coalition has continued its work to this day to improve relations between different racial/ethnic groups, sexual orientation groups and religious groups through educating the public on the issues of racism, sexism, homophobia, antisemitism, and islamophobia. They had successful rallies in response to the Charlottesville white nationalist rally where one person was killed in 2017 (Figure 46), in support of immigrant rights in 2018, and in response to the acquittal of the policeman who killed Antwon Rose in Pittsburgh in 2019 (Unity Coalition Website, 2018, WJAC TV, 2019). The coalition is still active and is run by Rachel Allen and Christine Dahlin.

Figure 47, The crowd at the Central Park rally in response to the Events in the Charlottesville, Virginia (panoramic photo)

Rosedale History Project

Cody McDevitt, a journalist for The Daily American, has written a book detailing the Rosedale incident of 1923 called Banished from Johnstown: Racist Backlash in Pennsylvania (2020). In addition, he has launched the Rosedale Oral History project. It attempts to chronicle the stories of those who were displaced from the city in 1923.

Put People First

Figure 48, Put People First Leadership Institute in Johnstown 2019

Put People First PA was founded in 2012 to give:
'...*voice to everyday people who are struggling to meet our basic needs. We define our basic needs as things we need to live healthy and fulfilling lives — things like education, housing, health care, jobs at living wages, food, and a healthy environment. (Put People First, 2020)*"

It was brought to Johnstown by Danelle Morrow in 2016 and then taken over by Madeline Burrows, Hope Weigle and Savannah Kinsey. They are working to revive Dr. Martin Luther King's Poor People's Campaign from the late '60s. They have ten strategies to make this a reality (Put People First, 2020):

- Our focus is on organizing the unorganized by base building. We build permanently organized communities.
- We make the invisible root causes of our conditions visible through education and action.
- For us, everyday people – not 'experts' – are the leaders. Leaders are not born, they are developed. Everything we do, we do to develop leaders.
- We are transformational, not transactional. Our organizing practice respects the whole person and the whole family.
- Our basic needs are our human rights. We use a human rights framework and five principles – universality, equity, accountability, participation and transparency- to guide our work and our organization.
- We are politically independent, and we hold all power holders accountable.
- We build leadership across difference – meaning our leaders are skilled at undermining oppression while uniting the majority across difference.
- We create own our own narrative and challenge dominant stories that prop up the status quo.
- We build solidarity across organizations and

movements. We show up for all struggling and oppressed people.
- We engage in grassroots fundraising, because funding our work ensures that we are accountable to our members and can set our own agenda.

Efforts to Reform the Catholic Church

In 2016, a Grand Jury was convened by the state Attorney General to investigate sexual abuse by clergy in the Altoona-Johnstown Catholic Diocese. This was precipitated by the scandals at Bishop McCort High School that were previously discussed. The small size of the Diocese's congregations made it easier to focus for a first state Grand Jury on this topic. The Grand Jury identified 50 clergy, mostly priests, who had molested children. Grand Juries were previously convened for the Philadelphia Archdiocese by the local District Attorney and were later convened for the remaining six Dioceses of the state. Table 12 shows the number identified in each diocese in the State with the raw numbers and adjusted numbers by Catholic population.

Table 12
Number of Abusive Priests Identified by Pennsylvania Grand Juries Adjusted for Population to Allow for Comparison Between Dioceses

Diocese	# of Abuser Clergy	Catholic population	Per capita abusers per 100,000	Grand Jury Year
Allentown	37	258,997	14.29	2018
Erie	41	221,508	18.51	2018
Harrisburg	45	230,000	19.57	2018
Pittsburgh	99	632,138	15.66	2018
Scranton	59	348,600	16.92	2018
Greensburg	20	137,641	14.53	2018
Philadelphia	63	1,188,225	5.30	2003
Altoona-Johnstown	50	98,284	50.87	2016
Statewide	414	3,115,393	13.29	

The table above shows that when adjusted for population, the Altoona-Johnstown Diocese had the largest number of offending clergy identified by the grand jury. This may be due to the 2016 grand jury being focused exclusively on this diocese which had the smallest Catholic population in the state. The 2003 grand jury in Philadelphia was run by the Philadelphia District Attorney's office who did not have the same resources as the state Attorney General. The 2018 Grand Jury was run by the state Attorney General and was focused on the remaining six dioceses in the state. They found a roughly equal number of abusers in each of the other dioceses when adjusted for population.

Figure 49, Shaun Dougherty attending a Vatican Conference on victims of sexual abuse by Catholic Clergy.

In response to the various grand juries my former classmate at St. Clements School in Johnstown, Shaun Dougherty, has come forward as one of the victims of the clergy. He has campaigned to get the statute of limitations on suing the church for compensatory damages for victims of abuse lifted in Pennsylvania. He has also campaigned for victims in other states as well as at the Vatican. Dougherty and another classmate of mine Brian Sabo, met with the priest who abused them, George Koharchik. The meeting was broadcast on CBS News (2018). He is now running for the state senate seat held by Republican Wayne Langerholc this year (Sutor, 2020).

John DeBartola

Figure 50, John DeBartola (left) lampooning Mark Pasquerilla as The Blues Brothers

John DeBartola has been a regular attendee at public meetings in the city, county, and the Greater Johnstown School District (GJSD). He has filed many right-to-know lawsuits to make local government more transparent. He was instrumental in exposing nepotism at the GJSD. He has run for Mayor of Johnstown and for City Council (Sutor, 2019a). He has advocated for Bill 5. Some elites in town see him as a pain but he is sincere at promoting transparency in local government.

Organizations Working to Improve the Health of Johnstown

There are several nonprofit organizations working to improve health outcomes in Johnstown. Conemaugh Health System is not included because it is now a for profit institution. Mental health organizations are included in this section.

1889 Jefferson Population Health Center

In 2017, the 1889 Foundation partnered with Thomas Jefferson University in Philadelphia to create the 1889 Jefferson Population Health Center. They conduct research into the health issues in town. The center is located in the Pasquerilla Building in Downtown Johnstown. They have a four-pronged approach to addressing the issues of the region (1889 Jefferson Population Health Site, 2019):

- "Identifying key factors that contribute to poor health outcomes in our region."
- "Develop strategies to improve our region's overall health and wellness."
- "Implement initiatives to support residents' health."
- "Evaluate results and make updates as needed."

On their website they have published newsletters on traffic safety in the area, on the relationship between diabetes and kidney disease, on dental health, and on other health issues in the area. They have partnered with the Greater Johnstown School District. They presented their research on community health priorities at the annual conference of the International Society for Pharmacoeconomics and Outcomes Research at Baltimore Maryland in 2018.

Highlands Health

Formerly the Johnstown Free Medical Clinic, Highlands Health was founded in 1998 to service those who were uninsured in the gap between eligibility for Medicaid, receiving health insurance through their jobs, and being able to purchase private health insurance through their jobs. The clinic was able to provide "doctor visits, medication, basic labs and x-rays" to patients who fell in this doughnut hole. According to their website, "In 2013, the Clinic reported 3400 patient encounters. Over 6,000 prescriptions were filled valued at approximately $2 million (2020)". After the passage of the Affordable Care Act, underinsured individuals who meet certain income requirements and are rejected by Medicaid are given services. These services include:
- Primary care services.
- Alternative Medicine.
- Diagnosis and treatment of medical conditions.
- Routine physicals.
- Health screenings.
- Testing and immunizations.
- X-rays, lab work and minor procedures.
- Specialist referrals.
- Case Management.
- Children's Care.
- Diabetic Eye Exam.
- Geriatrics Health.
- Free medication upon examination (excludes narcotics).
- Medication management and education.
- Narcan distribution and training.
- Medication refills.

Hope 4 Johnstown

Hope 4 Johnstown was created in 2017 in response to a wave of deaths of children due to violence in the city (Hope for Johnstown, 2019). They propose a Cure Violence program to work to alleviate the "inequalities that have created a climate of violence" here in Johnstown. This is done by holding events for the youth of the city. The Cure Violence program claims success in Chicago, Baltimore, and South Africa by curbing homicides.

Cambria County Drug Coalition

The Cambria County Drug Coalition was founded to coordinate drug treatment and prevention efforts in the county. As previously stated, the county has the second highest drug overdose rate in the state from 2015 to 2018. The coalition was created in 2016 in response to the opioid epidemic. It is a consortium of healthcare providers, law enforcement, education and county government. According to their website they offer a reward of up to $5,000 for reporting drug dealers to law enforcement. They run three prevention programs in the schools including "Botvin Life Skills Training", "Too Good for Drugs", and "This is (Not) About Drugs." According to Guidestar, they have $161,041 in gross receipts and $44,320 in assets.

ACRP

Alternative Community Resources Program (ACRP) was founded to replace the City-County Clinic to provide mental health and educational services in four counties. It is run by current Johnstown mayor Frank Janakovic. ACRP runs an alternative school for children with behavioral problems. It was founded in 1989. According to Guidestar it has $12,099,811 in gross receipts and $6,523,614 in assets.

New Day Inc.

Founded in 1979, New Day provides Christian social services in Johnstown. These services include counseling, children and youth, family ministry, and outreach services. It is run by Rev. Jack Rupert. According to Guidestar it has $478,545 in gross receipts and $1,443,387 in assets.

Mom's House

Mom's House was founded as a place where single expectant mothers with unplanned pregnancies can stay if they do not plan to have an abortion. They receive training and services such as daycare and educational services. In return they sign a written contract where they are expected to:
- Attend school regularly.
- Maintain passing grades.
- Give three hours of service time per week to Mom's House®.

It was founded by Peg Luksik who ran several times for governor and lieutenant governor of Pennsylvania.

The Art Scene in Johnstown

One of the assets Johnstown has for artists is it has a low cost of living. There have been efforts to support local artists and to hold events to attract buyers for the artist's works. There are three centers to showcase and support local artists in Johnstown.

The Community Arts Center of Cambria County

Figure 51, The Stutzman Log House (1834) was the site of the original Cambria County Community Arts Center

In 1968 the Cambria County Community Arts Center (CCCAC) was established at the Stutzman log house in Westmont. To meet the needs of a growing arts community, the Goldhaber-Fend Fine Arts Center was later built to accommodate an art gallery, a museum of precious porcelain dolls, and classrooms for art classes. They have an annual Log House Arts Festival every Labor Day weekend with more than 100 vendors. According to Guidestar, in 2017 they had $1,959,987 gross receipts and $3,100,567 in assets.

Bottle Works Ethnic Art Center

Figure 52, The Bottle Works Ethnic Arts Center paying homage to the Tulip Bottling Company

In 1993 the building that housed the Tulip Bottling Company in Cambria City was purchased to create an art center where artists in different genres could practice their crafts. The Bottle Works Ethnic Arts Center now has six in-house artists who can make and exhibit their crafts. It now hosts a variety of exhibits, classes, and concerts. It is located on 411 3rd Ave in Cambria City. According to Guidestar it has $370,384 in gross receipts and $1,571,266 in assets.

Venue of Merging Arts (V.O.M.A.)

Figure 53, An outdoor concert at VOMA

Right across the street from the Bottle Works is the Venue of Merging Arts (VOMA) on 305 Chestnut St. Located in the old St. George Serbian Church, VOMA is more volunteer run than the Bottle Works. In the basement they have a cabaret theater for intimate concert events. On the second floor where the church used to be, there is a room that can be used as an art gallery or as a theater. According to Guidestar, VOMA has $36,758 in receipts and $34,802 in assets.

Historical Restorations in Johnstown
Roxbury Bandshell

Figure 54, A Concert at the refurbished Roxbury Bandshell

Roxbury Park used to be known as Luna Park (Whittle, 2005) before it was bought by the city in 1921. It once had a lake that was used for ice skating and had a horse racing track. In the 1930s it was replaced by Roxbury Park. The Roxbury Bandshell was built in 1939 for outdoor concerts by the Civilian Conservation Corps under the New Deal. In the 1970s, the bandshell fell into disrepair. By 2005 the city announced plans to demolish it. Citizens in the city organized to save it. The Roxbury Bandshell Preservation Alliance raised the money to renovate it. They now have regular concerts there in the summer. According to Guidestar they have $55,993 in receipts and $404,483 in assets.

Restoration of the Clara Barton House

Figure 55, The current state of the Clara Barton House

In the aftermath of the 1889 flood, Clara Barton, the founder of the American Red Cross, set up a makeshift headquarters at 662 Main St in the city. She used it to coordinate the distribution of aid to victims of the flood. Like the Roxbury Bandshell, it has fallen into disrepair in recent years as can be seen in Figure 54. Local contractor David Santa has organized Clara Barton House and Garden Inc, to restore the house as an important historical site. As they were in operation for only a few months before this writing they have not yet reported any assets on Guidestar.

Johnstown Area Heritage Association

The Johnstown Area Heritage Association (JAHA) was created in 1972 to preserve historic sites in the area. It runs the Flood Museum, the Heritage Center, which gives visitors a simulation of the experience that immigrants had in the early part of this century in Johnstown, and other historical sites throughout the city. They also maintain archives of records for the area. They have been very helpful in researching this book. According to Guidestar they have $1,035,430 in gross receipts and $9,060,540 in assets.

Tranquility Gardens

Figure 56, Some of the statues at Tranquility Gardens

Created by Serbian immigrant Stephen Purich as an homage to great Eastern and Western philosophers, Tranquility Gardens is now being developed as a place of reflection and learning about the great thinkers of our time. Purich has donated it to the Community Foundation of the Alleghenies as a community mentoring intervention program. It is in Menoher Heights off of route 271. Tours are given by appointment. In time it will be open to the public for tours.

XII. A SOCIAL MEDIA PROFILE OF JOHNSTOWN

Facebook, Twitter, and other social media are increasingly the space where ideas are communicated and debated. Looking at the popular pages and groups where the city is the primary focus can provide insight as to which issues are most relevant to the city among current residents and expatriates. It also gives an indication as to the image that outsiders see of the city. In this chapter, I will look at the popular webpages, at Facebook groups and pages, and at Twitter accounts where these discussions take place.

Major Websites about Johnstown

The website *Vintage Johnstown* by Lisa Cacicia began in 2010 and shows a lot of old photographs, advertisements, and newspaper articles from the city's past. The five most common topics of her posts are World War II newspapers (828 posts), trolley pictures (423 posts), downtown Johnstown (389 posts), a diary from 1947 (354 posts), and stores (287 posts). The web traffic counter at the bottom of the page says it has received 1,670,775 visits. This book takes a different approach.

I don't have any specific information on which websites are most popular in Johnstown but I do have information on how popular my website, CSI without Dead Bodies (the title is a pun on the TV show CSI), is in Johnstown using Google Analytics. From when I returned to Johnstown in March 2016 until the time of this writing (June 28, 2019) my site had 688 unique users in the city, 6.1% of total users. These users had 1,161 sessions on the site or 9.1% of total sessions. There were more sessions in Johnstown than any other city over this period. Some of the data for this book originally appeared on my website.

The site bounce rate of a site is the percentage of

times someone almost immediately leaves a site after arriving at it on the web browser. For this site it was 42.3% in Johnstown while it was 51.9% for the all of the site's traffic for this period. The users visited an average of 3.84 pages per session in the city. The overall average for this period was 2.61 pages per session. The average length of a session was two minutes and 32 seconds.

The most popular post on my site in Johnstown was the one profiling the number of documentary filmmakers who have visited the city since the 2016 election. The second most popular post was a recent post featuring a documentary on African Americans in Johnstown (Williams, 1992). The third most popular post was the one revealing that Hillary Clinton had won the city while losing the county. The fourth most popular post detailed how losses in registered Democrats have accelerated since 2016. The fifth most popular post was on the high percentage of the McCort graduating class in recent years who were in the National Honor Society.

Popular Facebook Groups in Johnstown

Now I'll take a look at the social media profiles of the city as in which Facebook groups are the most popular and where current and former Johnstowners go to discuss the issues related to the city. First, I need to describe the difference between a Facebook page and a group. A group is a space where members can post things relevant to the group's definition and other members can comment. A page is an entity on Facebook where only the admins can post but those who like the page can comment.

The Facebook group *Vintage Johnstown Memories* is run by the aforementioned Lisa Cacicia, Debra Orner, and Kelly Edwards. It has 15,619 members as of this writing and was created in 2012. The group's 'about" section states that it is "A group dedicated to preserving the memories of Johnstown and the surrounding area. I reserve the right to delete any posts that show others in a negative light. This group is set up for you to be able to post your own memories of growing up in Johnstown - without the fear of being picked on or made fun of....so please feel free to consider this a safe playground to play on..."

The Facebook group *Revitalizing Johnstown* has 3,850 members as of this writing. It is administered by Joseph Taranto, Lonnie Rietscha, and Dan Stonebrook. Its stated purpose is "for the mature discussion of issues concerning the City of Johnstown. Intelligent argumentation is encouraged, childish behavior is discouraged". It has existed since 2013.

The Facebook group *A Change for Johnstown* is another forum for discussion on the city. The main topic discussed is the urban blight caused by so many abandoned houses. It has 1,666 members and is run by Adam Kozlowski, Shawn Conrad, Joe Warhul, and John Swanson. It has been active since 2014. Their "about" section states that "This page is for people to vent about the problems in Johnstown Pa it will contain political discussion AND political satire."

The Facebook group *Positively Johnstown* was created in 2017 and has 2,810 members. It is run by Karina Perkosky, Paula Tomko, and Susan Costlow. Their site states "Welcome to a group that's actually interested in improving the Greater Johnstown region. Share what you're doing to make our community a better place! Keep discussion positive, respectful, and forward thinking."

The group *Johnstown PA Area Overdoses and Information* is" ...to collect information on the heroin and overdose epidemic in our city! This page isn't a solution to the overdose problem, it's a way to come together to discuss what we can do to try to help..." It has 3,778 members and is run by Milissa Teeter and Sara Heider Fabrizio. It was created in 2016.

The group *Johnstown Area Scanner Alert System Page*

has 16,369 members and is a place for discussion of what is said on the Police and Fire department scanner in the city. It is administered by V. Mike Santacroce and Lorraine McKissick. It was created in 2016.

The most popular group in the city is *Johnstown Trading Post (JTP): Local Buy, Sell, Trade group for individuals*. It is run by Kimberly Felan and has 18,720 members. It is a virtual flea market for the city and was created in 2011.

Twitter and Other Social Media

A search of Twitter accounts turned up a wide variety of usernames. Some of the more popular accounts were *The Tribune-Democrat* (@TribuneDemocrat, 6,691 followers), the Johnstown Police (@JTownPD, 2,979 followers), The Johnstown Flood National Memorial (@JohnstownFldNPS, 6,523 followers), *WJAC-TV* (@WJACTV, 17,540 followers), the Flood City Music Festival (@FloodCityMusic, 2,203 followers), *The Johnstown Area Heritage Association* (@JAHA, 2030 followers), *The Johnstown Tomahawks* (@JohnstownHawks, 6,439 followers), Pitt-Johnstown or UPJ (@PittJohnstown, 3,780 followers), and the *Cambria County War Memorial Arena* (@WarMemorialAren, 2,003 followers). I limited this list to those with two thousand or more followers. Of these *WJAC-TV* was the most popular. For comparison, *WTAJ TV* in Altoona which broadcasts in Johnstown had 13,420 followers.

Johnstown has a subreddit on Reddit.com with 649 members. A subreddit is similar to a group on Facebook for a given topic. There the all-time top posts are mostly nostalgic about the city's past or venting about something in the present. This is the only subreddit about the city on this site. The six top posts of all time there were:

1) On net neutrality

2) A nightime photo of Johnstown

3) A new bike shop in the city

4) A photo taken at a Pittsburgh Pirate game discussing the closure of Coney Island, a popular hot dog place.

5) This image

137

6) A profile of Johnstown native Steve Ditko.

Johnstown native, Steve Ditko, legendary comics writer and artist and co-creator of Spider-man and Doctor Strange, died at 90.

On Pinterest the message board Johnstown & Surrounding Area of Cambria Co PA has 1,010 followers and 336 pins. There are several boards labeled Johnstown, PA which have hundreds of followers and pins. A pin on Pinterest is similar to a post on Facebook or a Tweet on Twitter.

On *YouTube* the most viewed videos about Johnstown are:

1) Surveillance: Deer crashes through windshield of Johnstown, PA CamTran bus & walks out front door 377,699 views

2) Johnstown Dam Disaster, 320,901 views

3) The Johnstown Flood of 1889, 147,956 views

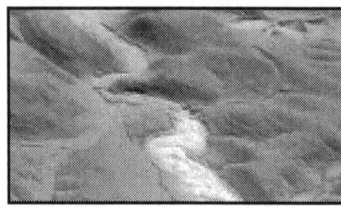

4) Johnstown-flood.mov, 111,128 views

5) Johnstown Flood 1977 TV Report, 98,011 views

6) Hatred at a Palin Rally in Johnstown, PA, 84,557 views

7) Trevy Is Famous "WHEN YOU'RE GONE" (Johnstown song), 48,618 views

8) Lacey Sturm w/ Third Day "Born Again" Johnstown PA, 2013, 43,553 views

9) Johnstown Flood Pa South Fork Dam Then/Now, 41,353 views

10) St. Bernard's Suffering in Johnstown, PA July 30, 2009: Thayne tries to get help for the dog, 38,650 views.

Five of the top ten videos are about the floods that the city experienced, four about the 1889 flood and one about the 1977 flood. Two are music videos. The top video is about something visually stunning. One is an appeal for help, and another is a political activist video. I posted Bruce Williams' (1992) documentary on African Americans in Johnstown on YouTube in May 2019. It has since received more than 1,000 views so it may make the list someday.

A search of the social content site Digg turned up these three posts.

1)

HORRIBLE BUT NOT SURPRISING
Donald Trump Is So Pumped For 9/11
29 diggs   Donald Trump   Politics   Photos   photo-blog-canvas   11 Sep 2018

@realDonaldTrump First Lady Melania Trump greet supporters as they arrive in Johnstown, PA to attend the Flight 93 September 11 Memorial Service in Shanksville, PA pic.twitter.com/SRMBvID...

2)

DRAINING MIDDLE AMERICA
In Towns Already Hit By Steel Mill Closings, A New Casualty: Retail Jobs
13 diggs   The New York Times   Economics   Internet   Human Nature   Long Reads   26 Jun 2017

After rebuilding, Johnstown eventually became prosperous from its steel and offered a clear path to the middle class.

3)

HE CAN DO NO WRONG
Johnstown Never Believed Trump Would Help. They Still Love Him Anyway.
12 diggs   POLITICO   Long Reads   Politics   Donald Trump   8 Nov 2017

JOHNSTOWN, Pa.—Pam Schilling is the reason Donald Trump is the president.

Households with Limited Access to the Internet in Cambria County

The *Restore PA* website shows the percentage of households in counties in the state with limited internet access. According to the map, Cambria County has 27.7% to 30% of households with this distinction. The county does not have the highest percentage in the state, but it does have a high percentage. The households driving the social media profile of the area in this chapter are likely part of the 70% or more of households with full access to the internet.

XIII. THE LITERARY SCENE IN JOHNSTOWN

One of the biggest surprises I saw since coming back to the city was the vibrant literary scene here in Johnstown and the surrounding area. I have met dozens of authors in the area who have written memoirs, poems, plays, and novels. Their work covers a wide variety of genres from science fiction, historical novels, self-help, biography, and history. They may not achieve the same notoriety as a J.K. Rowling, David McCullough, Malcolm Gladwell, or J.D. Salinger but they collectively make a statement about the area.

This is a brief summary of the authors of whom I am aware. I have met several other aspiring authors. The authors are presented in groupings of fiction, nonfiction, and poetry. The ratings on the websites *Goodreads* of the author and *Amazon* of their most popular book are reported when available and there are 20 or more ratings. The cover art is presented for books where I received permission to use it.

As the city economy and population declined, the only bookstores in Downtown Johnstown were *Inclined to Read,* a used bookstore in the Cambria County Library, *Chameleon* on the edge of Central Park, and bookstores at the Johnstown Heritage Association and the Flood Museum. A new bookstore and coffee shop just opened downtown called *Classic Elements.* In the Galleria Mall the only bookstore is *Books-A-Million.*

Fiction Books

Charles A. Taormina has published three books including *Gratuity* (2006), plays, short stories, and photography books. His three books on Amazon and Goodreads have no ratings. His play *The Dancer Within* has been performed at VOMA (Venue of Merging Arts).

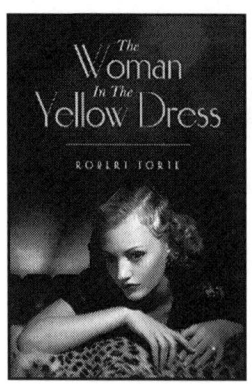

Robert Forte has written three detective novels and 30 screenplays. His most popular book is *The Woman in the Yellow Dress* (2016) which is in the Film noir genre. It has an average rating of 4.11 out of five stars on 19 ratings on Goodreads while on Amazon it has an average rating of 4.8 out of five stars on 22 ratings. He has sold two screenplays to studios that are awaiting a producer.

Ruschelle Dillon has written short stories in the horror genre with five distinct works on Goodreads. She has an overall rating of 4.38 out of five stars on 21 ratings. Her book *Arithmophobia* (2017) is a collection of nine short stories. She also has a blog where she posts poems and interviews with other authors.

Many books have been written about the Johnstown flood of 1889 with David McCullough's (1968) being the most famous. Local author Richard A. Gregory has written a historical novel called *The Bosses Club* (2011). It details the technical innovations at the Cambria Iron works and the events leading up to the flood. It has a rating of 3.88 stars out of five on Goodreads on 24 ratings. He is now working with Robert Forte on adapting the novel as a screenplay.

Joe Moore has written two children's books on the character Maxwell the Raindrop. He has two books: Maxwell: *The Raindrop Who Wouldn't Fall* (2014) and *Maxwell, the Raindrop: Am I Still Me?* (2015).

Timothy Van Sickel has written six books in a series called *Righteous Survival*. It is an apocalyptic fiction series. On Goodreads he has an average rating of 4.71 out of five stars on 72 ratings for all of his book listed there. On Amazon the third book in his series Righteous Sacrifice (2017) has a rating of 4.7 out of five on 21 ratings.

Tom Getty has written books in the horror genre and on filmmaking. He is a filmmaker as well as an author who has produced and directed Emulation and Rising Fear and has a book called *The Invading* (2017).

Kecia Bal won a master class to co-write a novel with renowned mystery writer James Patterson. *The Dolls* (2017) has an average rating of 3.46 out of five stars on 2,090 ratings on Goodreads. On Amazon it has an average rating of 3.7 out of five stars on 169 ratings. It is a story of female robots who kill.

Robin Strachan is a local freelance writer who has written for the *Tribune-Democrat* and *Johnstown Magazine*. She has also written three novels. On Goodreads she has an author rating of 4.1 out of five stars on 40 ratings.

Dorothea Ford has written a children's book *A Beach-Day Party* (2019). It has a rating of five out of five on Amazon on one rating. On Goodreads she has a one rating of five out of five for her book *Hide 'n' Seek: An Anthology... Hide 'n' Seek: An Anthology Depicting Predator and Prey* (2017).

Sally Fink has written four books in science fiction/fantasy.

Sandra L. Wirfel has written a children's book The Happy Cow (2013).

Michael L. Russo has written a religious book on Jesus Christ called The Via Dolorosa (2013). It has won a Christian Writers Award.

Beth Y. Lambert has written a religious novel called *The Harvester Chronicles: JP Knights* (2015). The novel is the first of a trilogy. The novel has no ratings on Goodreads or Amazon but a filmmaker, Kevin McAfee, is interested in adapting it for a movie (Hurst, 2019b).

Michele Mikesic Bender has written a humorous memoir MsGeezerette's *Journey Thru Baby Boomer Land at the Speed of Wrinkles* (2019).

The Rev. Dr. William G. Griffith has written the religious memoir *A Testimony: A Spiritual Adventure Retold* (2017).

The fiction authors who did not give permission to use their cover art are listed here. L.E. Martin has written a series of two romance novels titled *Laying it Bare*. On Goodreads, she has an overall rating of 4.92 out of five stars on 26 ratings. On Amazon, the first book in her series, *Laying it Bare with a Friend Request* (2019) has a rating of 4.9 out of five stars on 20 ratings. Peter Rhaven has written a book called *Strange Commotions: The Release of Dreams* (2009). It is a psychological journey according to the author in the vein of The Twilight Zone and the Outer Limits. Kristy Baxter contributed to the anthology of short stories, *The Binge-Watching Cure* (2018). Baxter wrote a story about the Johnstown Flood. Lisa Paolillo has written a romance novel called *What Happened in Vegas* (2015).

Nonfiction Books

Carlton Haselrig was a state champion high school and collegiate national champion wrestler who was drafted by the Pittsburgh Steelers as an offensive lineman. He went on to be selected to the Pro Bowl but later lost everything dealing with his personal demons. His book, *The Giant Killer* (2019), (co-written with Kevin Emily) details his story.

James and Suzanne Gindlesperger have written ten historical books and novels on the Civil War. Their top-rated books are on the Battles of Gettysburg *(So You Think You Know the Battle of Gettysburg vol. 1 & 2 (2010))* and Antietam (*So You Think You Know the Battle of Antietam (2011)*). Their books have an average rating of 3.92 out of five on 72 ratings on Goodreads and their book on Gettysburg (vol. 1) had an average rating 4.4 out of five on 37 ratings on Amazon.

Robert Jeschonek has written several nonfiction and fiction books. His nonfiction books recreate the feeling of being in the old Glosser Brothers and Penn Traffic *(Penn Traffic Forever (2016) pictured above)* department stores and in the old Richland Mall. Many of his fiction books are contributions to science fiction anthologies. On Goodreads he has over 109 distinct works with an average rating of 4.22 out of five stars on 407 ratings. On Amazon his book on *Long Live Glossers: A Department Store History* (2014), has a rating of 4.5 out of five stars on 20 ratings. He has won the Forward National Literature Book Award for *My Favorite Band Does Not Exist* (2011) and other awards for other books. He may be the most prolific author in the area.

Marianne Spaminato (2018), a writer for The Daily American, has written a memoir of her experience growing up in Johnstown in Listen to Your Mother: Reflections of a Baby Boomer with a Wonderfully Wise Mother.

Shelly Kerchner has written an autobiography on her struggle with an abusive husband and with a physical disability called *Standing Tall* (2017). On Amazon her book has a rating of 4.9 out of five on 20 ratings.

Becky Buchko has written seven books in the romance and self-help genres.

Betty Fieser Rosian is a long-time president of the local Christian Writers Group. Her book *What's a Grandma To Do?* (2016) has no ratings on Goodreads.

Brad Clemenson and Jim Penna wrote a biography of Congressman John Murtha called *Murtha: War Fighter* (2012).

Charles E. Kupchella has written five books on human evolution and morality. His most popular book on Amazon is *Morality: How it Evolved, How it was Hijacked and Confounded by Religion* (2019).

William R. Brice has written two books on the history of the oil and gas industry, one is called *Myth, Legend, Reality: Edwin Laurentine Drake and the Early Oil Industry* (2009).

As a 19-year-old on the Penn State-Altoona Campus, Michael Kiel was shot in the neck rendering him paralyzed from the neck down. His story is retold in *Challenge the Moment* (2019). On Amazon his book has an average rating of 5 out of five stars on 68 ratings.

Lori Vuckovich has written *Awakening Within the Dream* (2015). It is a spiritual self-help book. I don't know if she is related to baseball player Pete Vuckovich.

Former Lieutenant Governor Mark Singel has written two books, one on his year as acting governor while Governor Casey was having a liver transplant called *A Year of Change and Consequences* (2016), and another on the radical Republican and abolitionist Congressman Thaddeus Stevens called *The Life and Loves of Thaddeus Stevens* (2019).

The nonfiction authors who did not give permission to use their cover art are listed here. Tony Piskurich has written about his father's service in World War II called *Letters from Dad* (2019). Lisa Dallape Matson has written a profile of the Italian author and painter Dante Gabriel Rossetti (2010). Dave Hurst (whose Tribune-Democrat articles are cited in this book) has written an historical book, *Pennsylvania's Allegheny Mountains: The First Frontier* (2009). Randy Whittle wrote a two volume history of Johnstown (2005 and 2007) after the great flood which is a valuable source for this book. *Johnstown: The Story of a Unique Valley* (1985) is another valuable source for this book. Mike Brosig wrote Ride the Waves of Ownership Change: *A Practical Guide on How to Buy, Fund, Build, and Sell a Business* (2017). Lyndee Jobe Henderson and R. Dean Jobe wrote a photographic anthology about Johnstown for the *Images of America* series (2004). Henderson has a rating of 3.27 out of five stars on 27 ratings on Goodreads.

Poetry

Kayla Pongrac has written books of flash fiction such as *The Flexible Truth* (2015) and poetry. On Goodreads she has an overall rating of 4.43 out of five stars on 23 ratings. She has no books on Amazon.

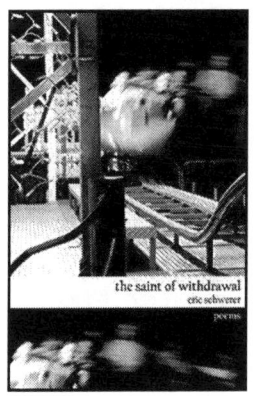

Eric Schwerer (husband of Kayla Pongrac) has written books of poetry such as *The Saint of Withdrawal* (2006). He is now leading a search for Johnstown's first Poet Laureate.

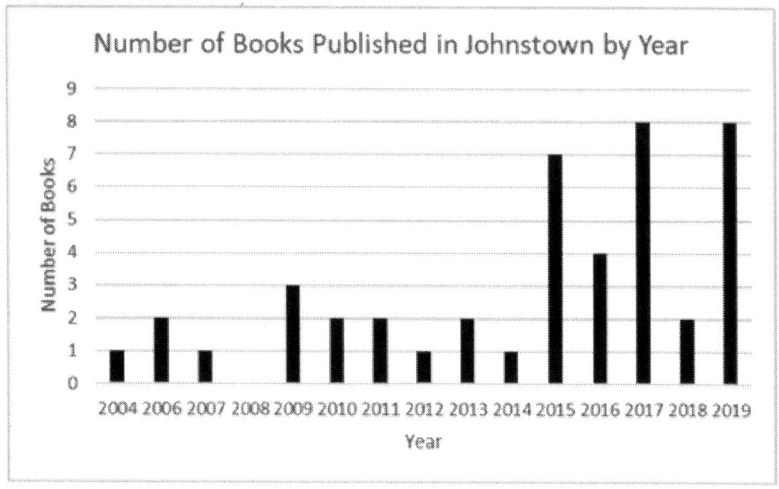

Figure 57, Number of Books Published in Johnstown by year 2004-2019 which are listed in this chapter.

This makes a total of 44 authors who live in the area (this author and book is not included in the total), 25 of them are men and 20 are women (the author of this book is not included in these numbers). There are authors who grew up here but moved away like Kathleen George who wrote *The Johnstown Girls* (2014), Russell Shorto who wrote *The Island at the Center of the World* (2005), and Steve Ditko (creator of Spider-Man) but this chapter focuses on writers who are here. They are good interpreters of what is going on here by either writing specifically on the city or being inspired by the events here.

Table 13 shows that while biography is the most popular genre (17% of the total) among local authors, followed by Religion/Spiritual at 14.9%, History and Science Fiction/fantasy/horror at 12.8%, and Children and general fiction at 8.5%) there is great diversity among them. Authors like Robert Jeschonek can write in more than one genre. All the books discussed in this chapter were written after the year 2000 except for

Johnstown: The Story of a Unique Valley (1985). The year 2017 was a prolific year for books in Johnstown with 8 published as seen in Figure 56.

Table 13
Count of Genres written by 44 Johnstown authors listed in this chapter.

Genre	Number	%
Biography/Memoir	8	16.7
Religious	7	14.6
History	7	14.6
Science Fiction/Fantasy/Horror	6	12.5
Children	4	8.3
General Fiction	4	8.3
Romance	4	8.3
Self Help	3	6.3
Nonfiction	2	4.2
Poetry	2	4.2
Historical Novel	1	2.1
Mystery	1	2.1
Total	49	100%

XIV. THE FUTURE OF THE CITY AND REGION

Most other books about Johnstown have been nostalgic about the city's past. These books were written mostly for those who have left the city. There are books about the Richland Mall and the old Glosser Brothers and Penn Traffic department stores by Robert Jeschonek. Others show old photographs from around the city. This book presents numerical slices of life in the city and surrounding communities from the early days up to the present.

Randy Whittle (2005 & 2007), Ewa Morawska (1985a; 1985b), Cody McDevitt (2019), and Donald Mitchell (1989) had extensively researched the city's past for their books. They were a big help in writing this work. This work is an update to their works on the city after the floods and the mills closed.

The city and its surrounding area have experienced a steady decline in population since the 1960s. Just this past April, the *Tribune-Democrat* (Hurst, 2019) published the most recent census numbers on population change in Greater Johnstown. While the region was not in the top three nationally in population loss as before, it did lose an additional 1% to bring it to 131,054 residents. This percentage loss was greater than neighboring Altoona (-0.6%), Somerset (-0.5%), and Dubois (-0.5%). Only State College (where Penn State is located) saw a net increase in the Central Pennsylvania at 0.3%. The disconnect between the city and its surrounding areas in poverty, demographics and political orientation more resembles the one that exists between Philadelphia and its surrounding counties.

Without a large infusion of capital, the area is unlikely to return to the glory days from 1920 to 1960.

It was easy for Trump to come here with promises of bringing the coal and steel jobs back. Those in the rust belt who voted for him in 2016 were giving the rest of the nation and the world a collective middle finger.

The *Tribune-Democrat* reports that the city government had a surplus for 2018 of $225,432 (Sutor, 2019b). This was the third straight year it had a surplus. The city now has $1,589,478 in its general fund.

Due to a new state law, the city will lose Act 47 protection for financially distressed communities in 2021 (Grass, 2018). This will make it more difficult for the city to run a surplus. The city has a total debt of $11 million and a pension liability of $25.7 million. The city also has a debt of $60 million for a sewer project that the state has mandated. The city collected 83.26% of real estate taxes levied in 2017. This is approximately 10 to 15% lower than surrounding municipalities according to Joel Valentine (Sutor, 2019f) who ran the audit that found the surplus. The report on the exit strategy for Act 47 makes these proposals (Grass, 2018):

1. The sale, lease, conveyance, assignment or other use or disposition of the assets of the distressed municipality.
2. Functional consolidation of or privatization of existing municipal services.
3. The execution, approval, modification, rejection, renegotiation or termination of contracts or agreements of the distressed municipality, provided, however, that the provisions of Section 252 shall apply to any Exit Plan adopted in accordance with this subchapter (section 252 provides limits on the ability of the plan to affect certain collective bargaining agreements or settlements).
4. Changes in the form of municipal government or the configuration of elected

or appointed municipal officials and employees as permitted by law.

The city and its surrounding municipalities can still be made a more pleasant place to live but any effort to reverse the fortunes of the area will have to address racial and income disparities which lead to the poor health outcomes. There has been an undercurrent of racism here much as there is everywhere else in the U.S. The hard part is to acknowledge this fact. There are some in the area making this effort such as the Unity Coalition and Put People First but more will be needed to bridge these divides.

The website *Planet Ware* rated Johnstown as the top-rated small town in Pennsylvania (Hamper, 2019) ahead of towns like Gettysburg and Lancaster. They cite the Flood Museum, the Heritage Center, the Southern Alleghenies Museum of Art, the Johnstown Symphony, and the Inclined Plane as reasons to visit the city. These rankings are often subjective, but any positive outside press is welcome. Amy Bradley (2019), president and CEO of the Cambria Regional Chamber wrote a column on this ranking in the *Tribune-Democrat* touting the new businesses in the area.

About the author

Paul Ricci is a statistician who was born in the Johnstown in 1970. He graduated from Bishop McCort High School in 1988 and from Indiana University of Pennsylvania in 1993. He moved away to Connecticut, Pittsburgh, and Utah for graduate school and work but moved back in 2016. He blogs at CSI without Dead Bodies (https://www.csiwithoutdeadbodies.com/) on a variety of topics related to statistics and society. He now teaches, consults, and works odd jobs in Johnstown. He is active in Put People First PA and other civic organizations.

References

1889 Population Health Center. (October, 2019).
> https://www.1889jeffersoncenter.org/.

Adler, B., & Doebereiner, S. (2018). *The binge-watching cure*. Claren Books.

American Lung Association. (2019). State of the air 2019: 20th anniversary.
> https://www.lung.org/assets/documents/healthy-air/state-of-the-air/sota-2019-full.pdf.

Associated Press. (2003). *Teacher drives student to Canada, dies from balcony fall.*
> http://www.bishop-accountability.org/news13/2003_03_07_AP_TeacherDrives_Thomas_Lemmon_1.htm

Associated Press. (1989). Pennsylvania county judge guilty of corruption.
> https://www.nytimes.com/1989/12/18/us/pennsylvania-county-judge-guilty-of-corruption.html.

BBC. (2016). World have your say.
> https://www.bbc.co.uk/sounds/play/p04f04lx.

Berger, K. Ed. (1985). *Johnstown: the story of a unique valley.*
Johnstown, PA, Johnstown Flood Museum.

Bishop McCort High School. (June, 2019). https://www.mccort.org/.

Bottle Works Ethnic Arts Center. (2019). http://bottleworks.org/.

Bradley, A. (2019). Vision 2025: Johnstown ranked No. 1 small town in Pennsylvania. The Tribune-Democrat. https://www.tribdem.com/news/vision-johnstown-ranked-no-small-town-in-pennsylvania/article_dac614fa-e26d-11e9-a9f9-4ba0006f7431.html?fbclid=IwAR3WhQRp2Xgfd2GbaAkO0XT-rOCrXkOYWFooks52zLj4PQ_QLa-Nei6B1bE.

Brice, W. R. (2009). *Myth, legend, reality: Edwin Laurentine Drake and the early oil industry.* Oil Region Alliance.

Brosig, M. (2017). *Ride the waves of ownership change: a practical guide on how to buy, fund, build, and sell a business.* Select Press.

Buchko, B. (2015). *How to talk to your dead loved ones: a short tale & easy instructions.* Single Parent Presse.

Johnstown Cafe. (2019). Burgesses and mayors of Johnstown. from
> http://www.johnstowncafe.com/johnstownhistoryjohnstownmayors.php.

Central Catholic High School Website. (2019).
> https://www.centralcatholichs.com/.

U. S. Census Bureau. (2018). *Quickfacts*. (2019, February 19), from https://www.census.gov/quickfacts/cambriacountypennsylvania.

Clemenson, B. & Penna, J. (2012). *Murtha war fighter: fighting for the soul of America*. Outskirts Press.

Coleman, N. (1985). History of Public Transportation. In K. Berger (Ed.), *Johnstown: The Story of a Unique Valley*. The Johnstown Flood Museum: 419-455.

Robert Wood Johnson Foundation. (2020). County Health Rankings. http://www.countyhealthrankings.org/

Capote, N., & Horner, C. (Director). (2018). *White Anxiety* (Season 1, episode 4) In Couric, K., & Condon, J. (Executive Producers) *America Inside Out*. The National Geographic Channel. https://www.nationalgeographic.com/tv/watch/79619204f9221f33917fa2ec4c98e168/.

Craig, J. M. (2014). *The Ku Klux Klan in Western Pennsylvania, 1921-1928*. Lehigh University Press.

CSI without Dead Bodies. (2018). *Losses in registered Democrats have accelerated since 2016 for Cambria and Somerset Counties (PA)*. https://www.csiwithoutdeadbodies.com/2018/10/losses-un-registered-democrats-have.html.

CSI without Dead Bodies. (2018). *NHS membership, not school year predicts prestige in college admission at McCort*. https://www.csiwithoutdeadbodies.com/2018/06/nhs-membership-not-school-year-predicts.html.

Dallape-Matson, L. (2010). *Re-Presentations of Dante Gabriel Rossetti: portrayals in fiction, drama, music, and film*. Cambria Press.

Bishop Accountability. (2014). *Database of priests accused of sexual abuse*. http://www.bishop-accountability.org/priestdb/PriestDBbylastName-B.html.

Dillon, R. (2017). *Arithmophobia*. Mystery and Horror.

Drug Enforcement Agency. (2018). *The opioid threat in Pennsylvania*. https://www.overdosefreepa.pitt.edu/wp-content/uploads/2018/10/PA-Opioid-Report-.Final.pdf .

Encyclopedia Brittanica. (2019). *September 11 attacks*. https://www.britannica.com/event/September-11-attacks.

Emily, K., & Haselrig, C. (2019). *The giant killer*. Self-Published.

Federal Bureau Investigation. (2019a). *Uniform crime report: UCR offense definitions*. https://www.bjs.gov/ucrdata/offenses.cfm.

Federal Bureau Investigation. (2019b). *Uniform crime report: UCR offensed definitions*. https://www.bjs.gov/ucrdata/offenses.cfm.

Fieser-Rosian, B. (2016). *What's a grandma to do?: 20 fun things to do with young grandchildren.* WestBow Press.

Fink, S. C. (2013). *Ten thousand gods (tales of the Lalloure, #1).* Self-Published.

Finnerty, J. (2019a). OD deaths dropped in 2018, but stimulant deaths rose. *The Tribune-Democrat.* https://www.tribdem.com/pennsylvania/news/state-od-deaths-dropped-percent-in-stimulant-deaths-rose article_67d48b4a-d29e-5c0e-9290-e4294f3138ba.html.

Finnerty, J. (2019b). From bondage to freedom: slavery lingered across Pennsylvania decades after practice abolished by law. *The Tribune-Democrat.* https://www.tribdem.com/news/from-bondage-to-freedom-slavery-lingered-across-pennsylvania-decades-after/article_6305fb62-1e6b-11ea-ac14-c76cbf12fdde.html.

Ford, D. (2019). *A beach day party.* Self-Published.

Forte, R. (2016). *The woman in the yellow dress.* Self-Published.

Fox, J. (2010). *Gasland.* HBO Documentary Films.

Furnary, S. & Zepeda, H. (2018). *With the rain.* Documentary for Oberlin College. https://vimeo.com/249275112.

George, K. (2014). *The Johnstown girls.* University of Pittsburgh Press.

Getty, T. (2017). *The Invading.* Acrolight Pictures.

Gindlesperger, J., & Gindleperger, S. (2010). *So you think you know Gettysburg?: the stories behind the monuments and the men who fought one of America's most epic battles.* Blair.

Gindlesperger, J. & Gindleperger, S. (2011). *So you think you know Antietam?: the stories behind America's bloodiest day.* Blair.

Battiste, N. (Writer). *Victims confront the priest they say abused them.* In Glor, J. (Editor) (2018). CBS Evening News. https://www.youtube.com/watch?v=HkEOxEvoO4c.

Grass, D. (2018). *City of Johnstown, Cambria County: exit plan pursuant to section 256 of Act 47.* https://dced.pa.gov/download/johnstown-city-act-47-exit-plan-adopted-11-1-2018/?wpdmdl=90142.

Grassi, V. (2019). *This Town Won't Die.* Scintillate Films. http://www.thistownwontdie.com.

Gregory, R. A. (2011). *The bosses club.* Self-Published.

Griffith, W. G. (2019). *Challenge the moment.* Self-Published.

Guidestar. (2019). https://www.guidestar.org/.

Hamper, A. (2019). 11 Top-Rated Small Towns in Pennsylvania. *Planet Ware.* https://www.planetware.com/pennsylvania/top-rated-small-towns-in-pennsylvania-us-pa-187.htm.

Highlands Health. (2020). http://www.highlandshealthclinic.com/clinic-statistics/.

Hurst, D. (2009). *Pennsylvania's Mlegheny Mountains: the first frontier (Regional Histories)*. History Press.

Hurst, D. (2019a). Data: Region's population continues to shrink. *The Tribune-Democrat*, https://www.tribdem.com/news/familiar-trend-data-show-region-s-population-continues-to-shrink/article_207d4140-695f-11e9-aeef-f34cae7e0fbb.html.

Hurst, D. (2019b). Filmmaker wants to turn Johnstown author's book into movie trilogy. *The Tribune-Democrat*. https://www.tribdem.com/news/filmmaker-wants-to-turn-johnstown-author-s-book-into-movie/article_33d3f3c6-9630-11e9-bd74-4340e16a2f94.html.

Hope for Johnstown. (2019). https://www.hope4johnstown.org.

Jeschonek, R. (2011). *My favorite band does not exist*. Clarion Books.

Jeschonek, R. (2014). *Long live Glosser's: a department store history*. Pie Press.

Jeschonek, R. (2015). *Penn Traffic forever*. Pie Press.

Jobe-Henderson, L., & Jobe, R. D. (2004). *Images of America: Johnstown*. Arcadia.

Johnstown Area Heritage Association (JAHA) Archives. (2017). *The unity coalition*. Johnstown, PA Website. from http://johnstownpa.com/history.html.

Johnson, H. B., & du Pont, B.T. (1985). The Black Community. In K. Berger (Ed.), *Johnstown: the story of a unique valley*. Johnstown, PA, The Johnstown Flood Museum: 529-588.

Johnson, G., Giles, E., & Michaels, M. (1985). *Johnstown and the Pennsylvania Canal*. In K. Berger (Ed.), Johnstown: the story of a unique valley. Johnstown, PA, The Johnstown Flood Museum: 211-254.

Kerchner, S. (2017). *Standing tall: the healing power of gratitude*. Readerplace.

Kerr, S. (2006). Preacher o' hate targets Johnstown gay bar. From *Pittsburgh Lesbian* https://www.pghlesbian.com/blog/GaythingstodoinPgh/_archives/2006/8/31/2281589.html.

Kiel, M. (2019). *Challenge the Moment*. Self-Published.

Kruse, M. (2017). Johnstown never believed Trump would help. They still love him anyway. *Politico*. https://www.politico.com/magazine/story/2017/11/08/donald-trump-johnstown-pennsylvania-supporters-215800.

Kupchella, C. E. (2014). *MORALITY: how it evolved, how it was hijacked and confounded by religion*. Self-Published.

Lambert, B. A. (2015). *The harvester chronicles:* JP Knights. Redemption Press.

Levine, M. (2006). New target, old methods for street preachers. *Pittsburgh City Paper.*

Marcus. M. (2002). Hate group activity slowing in region, FBI official says. *The Tribune-Democrat.*

Martin, L. E. (2019). *Laying it bare with a friend request.* Self-Publish.

McCullough, D. G. (1968). *The Johnstown Flood.* New York, Simon & Schuster.

McDevitt, C. (2017). Oldest black church in Johnstown has led the way on Civil Rights. *Daily American.* https://www.dailyamerican.com/entertainment/oldest-black-church-in-johnstown-has-led-the-way-on/article_d64bb3b5-0080-5279-a060-c827ed799655.html.

McDevitt, C. (2020). *Banished from Johnstown: racist backlash in Pennsylvania.* The History Press.

Measure of America. (2013). *The measure of America, 2013-2014.* http://measureofamerica.org/measure_of_america2013-2014/.

Mikesic-Bender, M. (2019). *MsGeezerette's journey thru baby boomer land at the speed of wrinkles.* Self-Published.

Mitchell, D. M. (1989). *A History of Homelessness- A Geography of Control: The Production of Order and Marginality in Johnstown, Pennsylvania.* Geography, The Pennsylvania State University. Master's.

Moore, J. (2014). *Maxwell: the raindrop who wouldn't fall.* Self-Published.

Moore, J. (2015). *Maxwell, the raindrop: am I still me?* Self-Published.

Morawska, E. (1985a). *For bread with butter: worlds of East Central Europeans in Johnstown, Pennsylvania, 1890-1940.* Cambridge University Press.

Morawska, E. (1985b). Johnstown's ethnic groups. In K. Berger, *Johnstown: The Story of a Unique Valley.* Johnstown, PA, The Johnstown Flood Museum: 486-524.

Musselman, R. (July, 2016). Hillary Clinton bus tour to stop in Johnstown Saturday, but event closed to public. *WJAC-TV.* Johnstown, PA. https://wjactv.com/news/election/hillary-clinton-bus-tour-to-stop-in-johnstown-saturday-but-event-closed-to-public.

OverdoseFreePA. (2019). http://www.overdosefreepa.pitt.edu/know-the-facts/view-overdose-death-data/.

Paolillo, L. (2015). *What happened in Vegas.* Smashwords Edition.

Patterson J., & Bal, K. (2017). *The Dolls.* Bookshots.

Pennsylvania State Data Center. (2019). *PA Crime Trend Data Dashboard.* http://pacrimestats.info/CrimeTrendDashboard.aspx.

Pennsylvania State Data Center. (2019). *Special Education Data Reporting.* https://penndata.hbg.psu.edu/Home/fbclid/

Pesto, M. (2017). Johnstown City Council approves new police chief, passes hate-crimes bill. *The Tribune-Democrat.* https://www.tribdem.com/news/johnstown-city-council-approves-new-police-chief-passes-hate-crimes/article_135109c6-517d-11e7-96ae-0775cab90396.html.

Piskurich, T. (2019). *Letters from Dad.* Daily American.

Pongerac, K. (2015). *The flexible truth.* Anchor & Plume.

Pritchard, R. (2019). Locals host vigil in honor of Antwon Rose. *WJAC TV.* https://wjactv.com/news/local/locals-host-vigil-in-honor-of-antwon-rose.

Put People First. (2020). Who We Are. https://www.putpeoplefirstpa.org/who-we-are/.

Remaking Cities Institute. (2015). *Johnstown vision 2025: A resilience framework.* https://issuu.com/cfalleghenies/docs/vision_2025_strategic_vision_with_a.

Rhaven, P. (2009). *Strange commotions.* Author House.

Roberts, D. (November, 2016). Voters in Johnstown, Pennsylvania, weigh in on election day. *ABC News.* https://abcnews.go.com/Politics/video/voters-johnstown-pennsylvania-weigh-election-day-43384700

Roddy, D. (1998). O'Kicki saga nears an end. *Pittsburgh Post-Gazette.* http://old.post-gazette.com/columnists/19980704broddy5.asp .

Roxbury Bandshell: The Original House of Rock. (2019). http://www.roxburybandshell.com/.

Russo, M. L. (2013). *The via dolorosa.* Xulton Press.

Pittsburgh Post-Gazette. (2002). 'All nine alive!' The story of the Quecreek Mine rescue. http://old.post-gazette.com/localnews/20020804all9indexp9.asp

Johnstown Area Heritage Association. (2003). Johnstown's Nineteenth Century African American History Primer. Johnstown, Pa.

Sauter, M. (2019). Across the U.S: What are the 35 poorest towns in America? *USA Today.* https://www.usatoday.com/story/money/2019/06/08/americas-poorest-towns-low-and- middle-income-families-left-behind/39552/791/?fbclid=IwAR3W6s6wL5sv9cbd7a6SVlJHbjhbsSNRMzxQukLSCtAc3KhZm_4jdIPFit0.

Schwerer, E. (2006). *The saint of withdrawal.* Wordtech Communications.

Sherman, R. B. (1963). "Johnstown v. the Negro: Southern migrants and the exodus of 1923."
Pennsylvania history: a journal of mid-Atlantic studies 30, 454-464.

Shorto, R. (2005). *The island at the center of the world: the epic story of Dutch Manhattan and the forgotten colony that shaped America.* Vintage.

Singel, M. S. (2016). *A year of change and consequences*. Sunbury Press.

Singel, M. S. (2019). *The life and loves of Thaddeus Stevens*. Sunbury Press.

Siwy, B. (2017). Texas researcher takes an interest in Johnstown. *Daily American*. https://www.dailyamerican.com/ourtownjohnstown/texas-researcher-takes-an-interest-in-johnstown/article_45fa0d26-77b8-11e7-91d7-97104f114779.html?fbclid=IwAR3I4sTxCBDbPJjXeNWCy2DD-GYBLUEbrV9o5eZm9uBZlye7AVqN85evS6Q.

Spaminato, M. (2018). *Listen to Your Mother*. Daily American.

Stanish, E. (December, 2017). 4 cases remain open in city after 10 homicides in Cambria County. *WJAC-TV*. https://wjactv.com/news/local/four-cases-remain-open-in-city-after-10-homicides-in-cambria-county.

Stebbins, S., & Sauter, M. (2019). The poorest town in each state. *Microsoft News*. https://www.msn.com/en-us/money/realestate/the-poorest-town-in-every-state/.

The Stonycreek River. (2008). From http://www.thestonycreek.com/about_ecology.shtml.

Strachan, R. (2015). *Designing hearts*. Camel Press.

Sojak, F. (2011). Santorum to enter race in region. *The Tribune-Democrat*. https://www.tribdem.com/news/local_news/santorum-to-enter-race-in-region/article_9660a51d-1525-54c2-bab9-731523c20a38.html.

Sutor, D. (2013). What would the Johnstown region look like with municipal consolidation? *The Tribune-Democrat*. https://www.tribdem.com/news/local_news/what-would-the-johnstown-region-look-like- with-municipal-consolidation/article_ea96b7f0-8e1b- 572d-8a40-c230737d5331.html.

Sutor, D. (October, 2016). 'Your jobs will come back': Trump talks Johnstown issues with War Memorial crowd. *The Tribune-Democrat*. Johnstown, PA. https://www.tribdem.com/news/your-jobs-will-come-back-trump-talks-johnstown-issues-with/article_b15f6ac6-97c5-11e6-9510-f73ca2536751.html.

Sutor, D. (2017a). Johnstown weighing Act 47 options. *The Tribune-Democrat*. https://www.tribdem.com/news/johnstown-weighing-act-options/article_849ba858- 2af3-11e7-b5d1-4b3693a0a030.html.

Sutor, D. (2017b). Focus on Race: Father expresses frustration at handling of son's murder. *The Tribune Democrat*. https://www.tribdem.com/news/focus-on-race-father-expresses-frustration-at-handling-of-son/article_1e403c78-ac9d-11e7-976d-cb6fe0e2f024.html.

Sutor, D. (2018). Warmer weather brings return of controversial sewer project.

The Tribune Democrat. https://www.tribdem.com/news/warmer-weather-brings-return-of-controversial-sewer-project/article_97de0000-46a4-11e8-bf3e-af6f1e89c97b.html.

Sutor, D. (2019a). DeBartola seeks city council position. *The Tribune Democrat.* https://www.tribdem.com/news/debartola-seeks-city-council-position/article_3fce40ae-4212-11e9-ba93-376377fc88f8.html.

Sutor, D. (2019b). City in Black for 3rd Straight Year. *The Tribune Democrat.* https://www.tribdem.com/news/audit-finds-johnstown-in-black-for-rd-straight-year/article_4a2a157a-a908-11e9-b1b2-fb781040f00d.html.

Sutor, D. (2019c). Williams, Stanton call for city manager's dismissal. *The Tribune-Democrat.* https://www.tribdem.com/news/williams-stanton-call-for-city-manager-s-dismissal/article_4fd5b6d4-9fa1-11e9-a2da-cb533eea562d.html.

Sutor, D. (2019d). 'Painful' effort causes friction as property work lags in Johnstown. *The Tribune-Democrat.* https://www.tribdem.com/news/painful-effort-causes-friction-as-property-work-lags-in-johnstown/article_d5d928b6-c16a-11e9-95dd-3f475391edfb.html.

Sutor, D. (2019e). From Bondage to Freedom | Underground Railroad carried many through region's communities. *The Tribune-Democrat.* https://www.tribdem.com/news/from-bondage-to-freedom-underground-railroad-carried-many-through-region/article_ec94539e-1f36-11ea-94b5-171bb6e76716.html.

Sutor, D. (2019f). Exiting Act 47: 'Difficult decisions' ahead: Johnstown faces two-year deadline for shedding 'distressed' status. *The Tribune-Democrat.* https://www.tribdem.com/news/exiting-act-difficult-decisions-ahead-johnstown-faces-two-year-deadline/article_964edd32-f872-11e9-9c9a-339c8505f9cb.html.

Sutor, D. (2020). Westmont man, a global victims advocate, announces bid for state Senate seat. *The Tribune-Democrat.* https://www.tribdem.com/news/westmont-man-a-global-victims-advocate-announces-bid-for-state/article_97f1a994-431d-11ea-a7b6-9b9b7e60ee5b.html.

Taormina, C. A. (2006). *Gratuity.* Self-Published.

Unger, M. (2014). Comparing Unconventional Drilling in Southwestern PA. *FracTracker Alliance.* https://www.fractracker.org/2014/09/swpa-drilling/.

Unity Coalition of the Southern Alleghenies. (2018). www.unitycoalitionsa.org.

Van Sickel, T. (2017). *Righteous sacrifice: righteous survival EMP saga, book 3.* Self-Published.

Venue of Merging Arts (VOMA). (2019). www.TheVoma.com.

Vuckovich, L. (2015). *Awakening Within the Dream*. LuLu.com

Williams, B., & Yates, M. (1985). Labor in Johnstown. In K. Berger (Ed.), Johnstown: The Story of a Unique Valley. *Johnstown, PA, The Johnstown Flood Museum: 589-643*.

Williams, B. (1992). *We'll Make the Journey*. Documentary. https://www.youtube.com/watch?v=HvFufDnvjhU.

Wirfel, S. L. (2013). *The happy cow*. Sound Impressions.

Whittle, R. (2005). *Johnstown, Pennsylvania: a history, part one: 1890-1936*. History Press.

Whittle, R. (2007). *Johnstown Pennsylvania: a history, part two: 1937-1980*. History Press.

WJAC-TV. (Jan, 2020). Local student receives full, $313K scholarship to Ivy League school. https://wjactv.com/news/local/local-student-receives-full-313k-scholarship-to-ivy-league-school.

Woodall, C. (2020). The 35 poorest towns in Pennsylvania. Penn Live. https://www.pennlive.com/news/2018/01/the_35_poorest_towns_in_pennsy.html?fbclid=IwAR1_oNCb0KQUKsDPhukrITjBml97FK2oGxwb7D_7pKsf6XXatyhjPMojIiw

Appendix A
Comparison of Women Owned Firms to All Businesses in Johnstown,

Appendix A

Comparison of Women Owned Firms to All Businesses in Johnstown, PA

Major Industry Group(SIC based)	Women Owned Businesses						All Businesses				
	Firms	% of Firms	% of Industry group	Sales and Receipts ($1,000)	% of Sales	Sales/ Firm	Firms	% of Firms	Sales and Receipts ($1,000)	% of Sales	Sales /Firm
All industries	3259		0.223	447,949		137	14603		8663607		593
Agricultural services, forestry, fishing, and mining	58	0.018	0.171	19,592	0.044	338	339	0.023	192863	0.022	569
Construction industries and subdividers and developers	122	0.037	0.064	35,987	0.080	295	1910	0.131	415874	0.048	218
Manufacturing	94	0.029	0.153	101,638	0.227	1,081	616	0.042	2064164	0.238	3351
Transportation communications, & utilities	114	0.035	0.111	12,238	0.027	107	1029	0.070	781349	0.090	759
Wholesale trade	35	0.011	0.069	66,079	0.148	1,888	510	0.035	988533	0.114	1938
Retail trade	855	0.262	0.292	151,825	0.339	178	2929	0.201	1879756	0.217	642
Finance, insurance and real estate industries (ex sub & dev)	205	0.063	0.175	16,298	0.036	80	1171	0.080	1003029	0.116	857
Service industries (exc membership org & private households)	1658	0.509	0.312	43,649	0.097	26	5317	0.364	1319143	0.152	248
Industries not classified	118	0.036	0.143	641	0.001	5	825	0.056	18896	0.002	23

Appendix B
Looking at NHS Membership and College Admissions Prestige at Bishop McCort High School

Year			NHS (%) n	NHS (%) y	Total
1988	College Rank	1 (1st tier: eg. Harvard, Stanford)	6(46.2%)	7(53.8%)	13
		2 (2nd Tier: State related PSU, Pitt, Juniata)	30(61.2%)	19(38.8%)	49
		3 (3rd tier: branch campuses, state owned schools UPJ, IUP, Lock Haven)	54(91.5%)	5(8.5%)	59
		4 (Community College)	9(81.8%)	2(18.2%)	11
		5 (Military)	11(91.7%)	1(8.3%)	12
		6 (Emplyed)	4(100.0%)	0	4
	Total		114(77.0%)	34(23.0%)	148
2016	College Rank	1 (1st tier: eg. Harvard, Stanford)	2(40.0%)	3(60.0%)	5
		2 (2nd Tier: State related PSU, Pitt, Juniata)	26(53.1%)	23(46.9%)	49
		3 (3rd tier: branch campuses, state owned schools UPJ, IUP, Lock Haven)	24(82.8%)	5(17.2%)	29
		4 (Community College)	6(100.0%)	0	6
		5 (Military)	1(100.0%)	0	1
		6 (Employed)	7(100.0%)	0	7
	Total		66(68.0%)	31(32.0%)	97
2017	College rank	1 (1st tier: eg. Harvard, Stanford)	1(14.3%)	6(85.7%)	7
		2 (2nd Tier: State related PSU, Pitt, Juniata)	20(43.5%)	26(56.5%)	46
		3 (3rd tier: branch campuses, state owned schools UPJ, IUP, Lock Haven)	12(60.0%)	8(40.0%)	20
		4 (Community College)	6(100.0%)	0	6
		5 (Military)	5(100.0%)	0	5
		6 (Employed)	3(100.0%)	0	3
	Total		47(54.0%)	40(46.0%)	87
Total	College rank	1 (1st tier: eg. Harvard, Stanford)	9(36.0%)	16(64.0%)	25
		2 (2nd Tier: State related PSU, Pitt, Villanova)	76(52.8%)	68(47.2%)	144
		3 (3rd tier: branch campuses, state owned schools UPJ, IUP, Lock Haven)	90(83.3%)	18(16.7%)	108
		4 (Community College)	21(91.3%)	2(8.7%)	23
		5 (Military)	17(94.4%)	1(5.6%)	18
		6 (Emplyed)	14(100.0%)	0	14
	Total		227 (68.4%)	105(31.6%)	332

Appendix C
2016 Election Results by Precinct in Johnstown

Ward	Clinton		Trump		Margin		Clinton win
	n	%	n	%	n	%	
11th Ward	98	51.9	84	44.4	14	7.5	Y
Kernville	152	60.8	91	36.4	61	24.4	Y
Prospect	170	82.1	34	16.4	136	65.7	Y
7th Ward	343	63.4	177	32.7	166	30.7	Y
17th Ward-1	184	50.7	159	43.8	25	6.9	Y
17th Ward-2	213	44.5	238	49.7	-25	-5.2	N
17th Ward-3	152	43.7	186	53.4	-34	-9.7	N
17th Ward-4	100	42.6	123	52.3	-23	-9.7	N
18th Ward	129	38.7	186	55.9	-57	-17.2	N
19th Ward	182	43.5	221	52.9	-39	-9.4	N
20th Ward-1	233	41.9	298	53.6	-65	-11.7	N
20th Ward-2	208	51.5	182	45	26	6.5	Y
21st Ward	97	35.9	166	61.5	-69	-25.6	N
8th Ward-1	34	51.5	26	39.4	8	12.1	Y
8th Ward-2	116	42.5	144	52.7	-28	-10.2	N
8th Ward-3	277	37	434	57.9	-157	-20.9	N
Cambria City	85	48.9	74	42.5	11	6.4	Y
Johnstown-Center-1	108	59.7	66	36.5	42	23.2	Y
Johnstown-Center-2	108	63.9	55	32.5	53	31.4	Y
Johnstown-Old Conemaugh	131	56	93	39.7	38	16.3	Y
Total	3120	48.4	3037	47.1	83	1.3	11

Index

1889 Flood 9, 11, 14, 129, 139
1889 Foundation 112,113, 122
1889 Jefferson population health center 122
1936 Flood 22, 23, 24
814 Worx 115
A Beach-Day Party 146
AAABA 31, 35 102, 103, 104
ACRP 124
Act 47 32, 43, 44, 46, 161
Affordable Care Act 69, 123
African American 13, 14, 15, 16, 27, 41, 58, 59, 73, 75, 93, 99
African Americans 13, 14, 15, 27, 30, 55, 56, 57, 59, 63, 68, 72, 73, 74, 75, 77, 79
aggravated assault 88, 91
air quality 47, 78
All the Right Moves 30
Allegheny Mountains 6, 7, 8, 156
Altoona Johnstown Diocese 47, 119, 120
Amazon 141, 144, 145, 146, 148, 149, 150, 151, 152, 154, 155, 157
American Community Survey 84
Anabaptists 35
Andrew Carnegie 9
Andrew Hawkins 35
Andrew Mellon 9
Arithmophobia 143
Army Corps of Engineers 23
Artrell Hawkins 31
Austrian 16
Awakening Within the Dream 155
Barack Obama 43, 95, 99

Becky Buchko 152
Bedford County 77, 98
Bernie Sanders 95, 96
Beth Y. Lambert 148
Bethlehem Steel 12, 23, 24, 28
Betty Fieser Rosian 153
Bill 5 103, 122
Bill Shuster 109
Bishop McCort High School 21, 35, 47, 48, 49, 50, 119, 170, 174
Bob Casey 32, 110
Brad Clemenson 153
Brent Ottaway 109
Bryan Barbin 99, 111
businesses   29
Cambria 8, 10, 12, 13, 29, 30, 32, 33, 34, 36, ,37, 38, 40, 41, 43, 46, 47, 53, 54, 55, 56, 57, 58, 60, 62, 62, 63, 64, 65, 66, 67, 68, 69, 70, 71, 72, 63, 76, 78, 79, 80, 81, 82, 84, 87, 88, 89, 91, 91, 96, 97, 99, 99, 100, 108, 109, 112, 113, 124, 125, 126, 134, 137, 140, 141, 143, 162
Cambria City 19, 24, 113, 126
Cambria County 85
Cambria County Drug Coalition 113, 124
Cambria County Library 141
Cambria County War Memorial Arena 26, 97, 134
Cambria Iron Works 8, 12, 13, 19, 143
Carlton Haselrig 31, 150
Carol Grove 50
Casa Nova 35 116
Catholic school   20, 21, 50

Catholics 20, 21
Census 8, 10, 13, 14, 15, 17, 36, 37, 41, 42, 85, 86, 87, 88, 160
Charlene Stanton 44, 105, 106, 107
Charles A. Taormina 142
Chiefs 32, 39
child mortality 57, 58
chlamydia 67
Civil War 8, 16, 150
Clara Barton House 129
Clearfield County 98
coal 7, 8, 19, 22, 25, 35, 79, 98, 161
cocaine 59
Community Foundation for the Alleghenies 111, 112, 113
Concurrent Technologies Corporation 34, 111
Conemaugh river 6, 10, 25, 35
Conemaugh Borough 19, 26
Conemaugh Indians 6
Conemaugh Memorial Hospital 58
Conemaugh River 6
consolidating 27
Coopersdale 10
County Health Rankings 52, 53, 54, 57, 63, 65, 66, 67, 68, 69, 70, 71, 72, 73, 74, 76, 79, 81
crime 45, 88, 90, 91, 114
Crown-American Corporation 32
CSI without Dead Bodies 97, 131
Daisytown 46
Dave Hurst 156
David McCullough 141, 143
David Santa 129
David Vitovich 105
Democratic 98, 99, 100, 105
diabetes 64, 122
Digg 140
Divine Mercy Catholic Academy 50
Donald Mitchell 11, 160
Donald Trump 98, 99, 100
Donato Zucco 43
Dorothea Ford 146
drinking excessively 65
drinking water violations 79
drug overdose 61, 64, 124
Drug overdose deaths 60, 61
Duke Lifepoint health care system 16, 18, 51
East Central European 15, 16, 18, 27
East Conemaugh 10, 19, 46
Economic Census 36, 37, 41, 42
Ed Cernic 98
Eddie McCloskey 23, 101
Education 21, 100, 106, 115, 116, 118, 123, 124
elementary schools 20, 50
Emulation 145
Eric Schwerer 157
Ewa Morawska 160
exercise opportunities 65
Facebook 83, 131, 132, 133, 134, 137
FBI 88, 90, 91, 116
fentanyl 59
fire department 45, 134

firearm 78
flu vaccines 73
food environment 64
fracking 39, 46, 47, 79
Fractracker 46, 47
Frank Burns 98, 110
Frank Janakovic 105, 124
Frank Pasquerilla 32
Franklin 10, 19
Franklin Roosevelt 23
Gary Younge 100
GasLand 47
Glenn Thompson's 109
Glosser Brothers 113, 151, 160
Goodreads 141, 142, 143, 144, 145, 146, 148, 149, 150, 151, 153, 156, 157
Great Depression 22, 23, 30
Greater Johnstown 16, 27, 36, 43, 59, 86, 91, 92, 93, 94, 102, 113, 121, 122, 133, 160
Grubbtown 10
Guidestar 48, 111, 113, 124, 126, 127, 128, 129, 130
Hanson brothers 28
Henry Clay Frick 9
Herb Pfuhl 27
high school graduation rate 74
Highlands Health 123
Hillary Clinton 95, 96, 98, 99, 132
Hispanic 41, 55, 63, 68, 72, 73, 74, 75, 80, 93, 94
HIV 67
Hockeyville USA 39

homicide 55, 58, 77, 88, 89, 91, 124
Hope 4 Johnstown 123
housing 24, 80, 118
How to Talk to Your Dead Loved Ones 152
Hungarian 16
Hunter Zepeda 101
Ideal Park 23
immigrants 8, 16, 17, 18, 19, 25, 130
Incline Plane 11, 12, 13, 23, 162
income 22, 24, 25, 44, 75, 85, 87, 123, 162
infant mortality 58
injury 77
International Ladies Garment Workers Union (ILGWU) 23
internet 115, 140
Italian 41, 156
Italian immigrants 14, 19
Jack Ham 31
Jack Williams 44, 105
James and Suzanne Gindlesperger 150
James Patterson 145
Jerry Carnicella 110
Jim Penna 153
Jim Rigby 110
Joe Moore 144
John DeBartola 105, 121
John Murtha 27, 39, 153
John Wozniak 98
Johnstown 6, 7, 8, 10, 11, 13, 15, 16, 20, 21, 22, 24, 26, 27, 28,

30, 31, 32, 33, 34, 36, 25, 41, 43, 46, 51, 52, 55, 59, 80, 81,85, 86, 87, 88, 90, 91, 92, 94, 95, 96, 98, 99, 100, 101, 102, 103, 104, 105, 106, 108, 109, 111, 112, 115, 117, 118, 122, 123, 124, 125, 128, 130, 131, 132, 133, 134, 137, 139, 141, 158, 159, 160, 173, 175

Johnstown Area Heritage Association (JAHA)   13, 14, 116, 130, 134

Johnstown High Schools   35

Johnstown Jets   28

Johnstown Magazine   145

Johnstown Redevelopment Authority   45

Johnstown School District   22, 26, 43, 86, 92, 93, 113, 121, 122

Johnstown Tomahawks   39, 134

Johnstown Tribune-Democrat   26, 60, 106

Joseph Adamec   47

Joseph Cauffiel   15

Joseph Johns   6

Joseph O'Kicki   32

Joseph Paul Franklin   30

Joseph Schantz   6

Katherine-Anne McCloskey   101

Kathleen George   158

Katie Couric   100

Kayla Pongrac   157

Kecia Bal   145

Keith Rothfus   43, 109

Ken Salem   50

Kevin Emily   150

KKK   20, 21, 35, 116

Korean War   26

Kristy Baxter   149

labor force   29, 30, 32, 33, 38, 39, 40, 41, 44, 52, 53

Larod Stephens-Howling   31

Lee Hospital   51

Lee Iaccoca   32

Life expectancy 55, 56, 57, 58

Lift Johnstown   112

Lilly   20

Linda Weaver   43

Lisa Cacicia   131, 132

Lisa Dallape Matson   156

Lisa Paolillo   149

Listen to Your Mother   151

Little Conemaugh River 6, 10, 35

Lori Vuckovich   155

Lou Barletta   110

low birthweight (LBW) babies   63

Luna Park   128

Lyndee Jobe Henderson   156

mammography   73

Marcellus shale   39

Marianne Spaminato   151

Marie Mock   105

Mark Pasquerilla   112, 121

Mark Singel   32, 156

Martella's pharmacy   104

Mason-Dixon Line 6
Maxwell: The Raindrop who Wouldn't Fall 144
median income 24, 87
Medicaid 69, 123
Medicare 71, 72, 73
Memorial Hospital 51
mental health 62, 71, 122, 124
Mercy Hospital 51
Mexicans 14
Michael L. Russo 147
Michele Mikesic Bender 148
Millville 10
Mom's House 32, 125
motor vehicle crash death rate 66, 77
Moxham 11, 21, 23
My Favorite Band Does Not Exist 151
National Drug Intelligence Center 34, 39
National Honor Society (NHS) 48, 49, 50, 174
New Day Inc. 124
Nunzio Johncola 105
Oakhurst 24
obesity 63, 64
opioid epidemic 58, 100, 124
Paul Newman 28
Peg Luksik 32, 125
Penn Traffic 29, 151, 160
Pennsylvania 7, 13, 16, 19, 20, 27, 31, 29, 41, 44, 42, 53, 54, 55, 56, 57, 58, 67, 81, 85, 86, 87, 88, 89, 91, 95, 102, 106, 117, 121, 125, 160, 162, 163
Pennsylvania Canal 7
Pennsylvania State Data Center 91
Pennsylvania's Allegheny Mountains: The First Frontier 156
Pete Vizza 105
Pete Vuckovich 31, 155
Philadelphia 7, 53, 60, 75, 77, 78, 95, 99, 119, 120, 122, 160
physical inactivity 65
Pittsburgh 6, 7, 9, 21, 35, 48, 49, 51, 52, 58, 60, 95, 99, 116, 117, 136, 150
Pittsburgh Steelers 31, 35, 150
Point Stadium 32, 35, 103
Police 15, 45, 50, 88, 89, 106, 134
poor physical health 62
poverty 74, 80, 85, 86, 87, 102, 160
preventable hospital stays 71
primary care physicians 69, 70
Prospect 10, 19, 24, 99
public housing 24
Put People First 117, 118, 162, 163
Quecreek mine 35
R. Dean Jobe 156
Randy Whittle 20, 156, 160
rape 88, 90, 91

real estate tax   44, 51, 161
Reddit   134
Republican   15, 27, 43, 96, 98, 105, 107, 108, 109, 110, 121, 156
Restore PA   140
Richard A. Gregory   143
Richland   16, 86, 92, 93, 94
Richland Mall   151, 160
Rick Santorum   19
Ricky Britt   105
Righteous Survival   144
Rising Fear   145
robbery   88, 91
Robert Forte   142, 143
Robert Jeschonek   151, 158, 160
Robin Strachan   145
Rolling Mill Mine   19, 20
Roxbury   11, 107, 128, 129
Roxbury Bandshell   128, 129
Roxbury Bandshell Preservation Alliance   128
Roxbury Park   128
Ruschelle Dillon   143
Russell Shorto   158
Sally Fink   146
Sandra L. Wirfel   147
Scott Wagner   110
segregation   75, 76
sewer   45, 46, 161
Shanksville   35
Shaun Dougherty   120, 121
Shelly Kerchner   152
Siobahn Furnary   101
Slap Shot   28, 29, 39

Slavic   16
Small Area Income and Poverty Estimates (SAIPE)   85
SNAP benefits   87
social association   76
social media   106, 131, 132, 134, 140
Somerset   19, 25, 36, 56, 60, 112, 116, 160
South Fork Fishing and Club   9
Southmont Boro   46
special education   91, 92, 93, 94
Standing Tall   152
State Supreme Court   108
Statistics   45, 53, 56, 61, 62, 81, 88, 91, 100, 111
steel   14, 30, 100
steel mills   32
Stephen Baker   50
Stone Bridge   10, 11, 35
Stonycreek   25, 35
Stonycreek River   6, 25
Strike labor   22, 23, 35
Sunnehanna Country Club   32
Susan Boser   109
Sylvia King   105
Teen Birth Rate   68
Ten Thousand Gods   146
The Boss's Club   143
The Bottle Works Ethnic Arts Center   126
The Daily American   117, 151
The Dolls   145

The Giant Killer 150
The Happy Cow 147
The Harvester Chronicles: JP Knights. 148
The Johnstown Democrat 126
The Johnstown Tribune 26, 60, 106
The Learning Lamp 111
The Saint of Withdrawal 157
The Tribune-Democrat 134, 145, 160, 161, 162
The Via Dolorosa 147
The Woman in the Yellow Dress 142
Thomas Lemmon 50
Thunder in the Valley 35
Timothy Van Sickel 144
Tire Hill 19
Tom Getty 145
Tom Wolf 110
Twitter 131, 134, 137
unemployment 22, 26, 29, 30, 32, 33, 37, 38, 39, 40, 52, 84, 114
Uniform Crime Report 88
uninsured 12, 68, 69
union 115, 116
United Mine Workers 8
Unity Coalition of the Southern Alleghenies 115, 116
UPJ 21, 134
US Steel 23
Venue of Merging Arts (VOMA) 127, 142
Vince Grassi 102
Vintage Johnstown 131, 132
Violent crimes 88
Vision 2025 113, 114
voter registration 97, 108
Wayne Langerholc 98, 121
Welsh 8
Westmont 16, 19, 20, 86, 91, 92, 94, 126
What Happened in Vegas 149
Windber 12
WJAC 26, 50, 110, 117, 134
Woodvale 10
World War I 14, 15, 22
WWII 26, 131, 156
years of potential life lost (YPLL) 54, 55, 57, 58
YouTube 137, 139